T0146814

Unpuzzling Finance

The Quick and Easy Way to Learn the Basics
of Finance for Non-Finance Managers

ZAHOOR BARGIR

authorHOUSE®

AuthorHouse™ UK
1663 Liberty Drive
Bloomington, IN 47403 USA
www.authorhouse.co.uk
Phone: 0800.197.4150

Published by AuthorHouse   06/24/2016

ISBN: 978-1-5246-2960-1 (sc)
ISBN: 978-1-5246-2959-5 (e)

Print information available on the last page.

This book is printed on acid-free paper.

Image cover design by Aneesa Dalwai and Pele Lazicic
and Photography by Nadia Butt

Contents

Part 1: The three basic statements

Part 2: Other elements of the basic fundamentals

Preface

One of the key things with finance is that it is just like any other subject. We simply need to find a way of learning that works for us. All too often, we find finance puzzling – if it is not the terminology that confuses us it is the numbers. In this book, we cover the basic concepts of finance along with financial terms to help you to become more familiar with the essential elements of this topic, and how each piece of the puzzle fits together. I am always being asked in the course of my work as a trainer, where to find a book that explains finance in an easy-to-understand way? This easy-to-read book introduces the fundamentals of finance in a straightforward manner.

During my school years I didn't find numbers easy to grasp and I was near the bottom of the class in maths. In fact, to cover up my lack of ability, I became the joker at the back of the maths class and made a fool of myself.

Surely, maths has got to be easier than this!

That was before I struck gold with Ian McDonald, a teacher who realised I didn't quite 'get it' and would sit with me to focus on just one thing – the process. He carefully showed me what to do and then got me to work through it myself. It was a revelation because he didn't confuse me with difficult terms or numbers; he concentrated on helping me understand the process involved, so that I could reach the right answer.

I soon began to apply myself and, with practice, achieved over 90% in my end-of-year exam. The euphoria I felt soon disappeared when I discovered I would have a different teacher the following year. But it dawned on me that even without Ian teaching me, I could apply the same methods to whichever mathematical problem I was faced with - because:

1) I had found an approach that worked for me

2) It was not so much about numbers; it was more about understanding the process

In this book I have taken the subject of finance and broken it down in a way that is accessible to anyone who is not comfortable with or, who has never studied the subject, like my maths teacher did for me.

Who is this book for?

Quite simply, it is for anyone who needs or wants to understand the fundamentals of finance.

Perhaps you own a business or are looking to set one up. Maybe you are working towards a promotion or want to develop your current role. You might be a chef who wants to understand how to price a dish with a view to making maximum profit. Whatever your situation, knowing about finance is invaluable. No matter what your speciality is, understanding the basics of finance will be crucial in both your professional life and your personal life.

This book is not intended to turn you into an expert, it will explain the basic concepts and how they work together. These essential first steps are explained in an easy-to-follow manner and aim to give you the confidence to learn more about finance.

Introduction

As a finance trainer, I've had the opportunity of working with thousands of people who have not found this subject easy. I have seen first-hand which techniques learners find effective and which areas people struggle with. As a result, in this book I focus on the core aspects of finance in two parts: firstly the three financial statements. When we assess a company to see how well it is performing financially, it is on the basis of these three financial statements, which we can consider as a simple collection of information on different aspects of running a business.

Part 1: The three financial statements consist of:

a. The Profit and Loss Account – This is information that helps us measure how good the organisation is at making money.

b. The Balance Sheet – This helps us keep a tally of all the assets that the business owns, and all the liabilities that it has.

c. The Cash Flow Statement – This highlights how much actual cash there is in the business.

The second part of this book will then focus on other aspects of finance that work together with the three financial statements.

Part 2: Additional financial elements include:

d.   Fixed and variable costs – When we make decisions that have a knock-on effect on other areas of our business, understanding costs will help us work out what the impact will be.

e.   Accruals – When we take a look at the finances of our business on a monthly basis, accruals play a major part in this. We will look at what they are and how they work.

f.   Budgeting – A budget is effectively a plan of where money is going to be spent. We will look at the components of a budget as well as how this compares to a similar plan, known as a forecast.

The three financial statements form the very cornerstone of understanding finance. They work together so that a business can make a profit and continue to trade. In Part 1 you will get a better grasp of the role they play.

In each of the sections, once the theory has been explained, there are examples to help you explore the financial concepts further. There are also questions, with answers, at the end of each chapter. The questions are not only a way of helping you to check that you have understood the concepts, but also to help you put the concepts into practice.

Acknowledgements

It was quite a journey to get this book to completion and it wouldn't have been done without the constant love and support of my parents and siblings – you are my world. I'm always running ideas by you, so thank you for your priceless suggestions and unstinting support. I also have a host of people to thank who have directly or indirectly made an impact on the production of this book.

Firstly, my teachers – Ian McDonald and Patrick Lynch. Whilst I struggled to find my learning style from a very young age, you inspired me to find a way and to appreciate my own talents. You have both been instrumental in my own training career.

Nothing is ever truly achieved on our own, and this book is certainly no exception. I wish to thank the following people for your excellent work and support in getting this to a finished product. A big thank you to my editor Teresa Palmiero for your great suggestions and professional guidance. You've been amazing in your support throughout and I really appreciate it. To David Frederick, my technical editor. You don't usually have much time to spare with all the teaching you do alongside your day job, so I really appreciate your expertise on this project. To my book designer Aneesa Dalwai who was so easy to work with as always and who knows how to convert ideas into an image. To my illustrator Pele Lazicic – it's our first assignment together and I couldn't have wished for a better cartoonist. I look forward to our future collaborations! To London House for their support, especially during those late nights in the library. To Nadia Butt for the photography. It is spot-on as always. To Debbie Thomas, for your eye for detail. Being a perfectionist, I'm not always one for keeping to deadlines, so thank you for your patience. And finally, to my friend and stand-by accountant, Imtiaz Haque. Thanks buddy, for being there whenever I've needed to throw out some accounting ideas, and other things at you.

I would like to thank the thousands of delegates I have had the privilege of delivering training to, as you have helped me grow and are the inspiration behind this book. And finally, I would like to thank all my colleagues who have been there for me throughout my professional life. It's been a fun and sometimes arduous journey, but I've learnt so much from you. Knowledge is to be shared and this is my way of spreading financial literacy to people who may never have seen finance as fun.

Thank you

Part 1
The three basic statements

Chapter 1

The Cash Flow Statement - *How am I managing my cash?*

Happiness is a positive cash flow – **Fred Adler**

Cash is the lifeblood of any company. In fact, cash is the very thing we all personally need on a daily basis, essentially to survive — to help us pay for our food, our bills, our everyday needs. A family may have a budget to help them understand how much money is coming into the household and how to manage what they spend. It isn't much different for a business or organisation. A Cash Flow Statement is what we use to manage the cash a company needs on a daily, weekly, monthly or yearly basis.

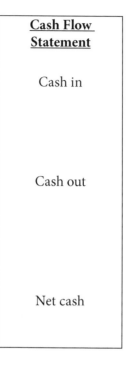

Figure 1.1: Cash Flow Statement

When it comes to finance, the Cash Flow Statement is one of the three main financial statements. In its simplest form, just like a family budget, this statement looks at cash coming into the business and cash going out. It's probably the most straightforward of the statements to understand but probably also the most important. As the adage goes, cash is King (or Queen) and this certainly is the case.

It is easy to remember what constitutes the Cash Flow Statement as it is basically the same format as your bank statement. A business needs to generate cash, to be more 'liquid', which means making sure you have the cash when you need it. If a business doesn't have enough cash, this can have serious implications on the performance of the business. If we have more cash coming in than going out, we are along the right lines.

A company can be worth a lot by holding plenty of assets, but if it does not have the cash to pay for everyday items, it will struggle.

The Cash Flow Statement is important because it helps you monitor how much cash you have which means a business has the freedom and flexibility to make decisions quickly. However, besides cash, a company also invests in assets to enable it to operate on a daily basis. Assets include: buildings, machinery, fixtures and fittings and so on. An asset is anything of value, which can be converted into cash. A company can be worth a lot because it owns plenty of assets. But to survive and succeed, it needs to have the cash available to pay for everyday items or it will struggle. For instance:

- You can have a building as an asset but that, in itself, cannot pay for the day-to-day costs of running a business. Many people find themselves in the position of having assets of huge value, like property, but without the cash to pay for daily things.

- You can have a warehouse full of stock but unless someone is going to buy it from you, this stock is just tying up your cash - which you could be using for something more important. So if you have paid £5,000 for stock which is currently left unsold, this is money you could be using for marketing or advertising.

Cash Flow Statement and your bank statement

So, someone may ask, if my Cash Flow Statement is like my bank statement, can't I just look at my bank statement for this information? Well, you can and your bank statement will certainly tell you how much money you have in your account. However, you may have several bank accounts, so instead of looking at each one separately, the Cash Flow Statement can give you the consolidated view, with them all added together.

Another reason why you would use a Cash Flow Statement, as opposed to merely looking at your bank account, is because the Cash Flow Statement makes the data more meaningful. Instead of looking at multiple transactions that have occurred for the purchase of stationery, you can save time and see this on one line in your Cash Flow Statement.

And this is why the Cash Flow Statement is important; it is a single source that is there to help us monitor, in a meaningful way, how much cash we have available to us within the business.

Exercise 1.1

Melissa's Cupcakes – Calculating a cash balance after six months of trading

CompanyBasix.com

Suppose you have been in business for six months and you want to see what your profit and cash look like? Here is a short case study for you to consider.

Melissa opened a cupcake shop (called Melissa's Cupcakes) on 1st July 20X1 and has invested £20,000 of her own money into it. She is renting the shop, has hired one full-time staff member as well as one part-time worker and purchased some equipment. She has also got a loan of £10,000 from friends and family, which is interest-free. Below is a list of her income (the money she has invested in the business as well as the money earned from sales of her cupcakes); and costs (the things she needs to pay for to get her business up and running) from July until end of December:

(Interest on loans is set at 7%)

Note: Throughout the book, costs will appear within brackets.

Other paid and unpaid transactions at end of Dec 20X1	
	£
Cash generated from shop sales of cupcakes.	10,500
Additional sales of £4,000 made from corporate customers. She has been paid £3,000 but she is still owed £1,000.	4,000
Rent for 12 months.	(3,600)
She has ordered £2,000 worth of raw materials (flour, sugar, cupcake paper cases etc.). She paid her suppliers £1,800 but still owes them £200.	(2,000)
She has used most of the raw materials she purchased but still has about £400 of untouched raw materials left.	(1,600)
She hired 1 full-time staff member at £15,000/year. Melissa has decided not to pay herself a salary for the first year of business.	(15,000)
She hired 1 part-time staff member at £5,000/year.	(5,000)
She bought equipment for £16,000. She paid for this up-front in one payment.	(16,000)
She paid the £10,000 loan back to friends and family.	(10,000)

Exercise 1.1: Calculate what the cash balance is for Melissa's Cupcakes (above) at the end of the six months up to the end 31ˢᵗ Dec 20X1.

Have a go at this exercise in the blank table below by inserting the different amounts for costs and income. The answer is underneath. The original investment of £20,000 and loan of £10,000 have already been inserted.

Cash in		Cash out	
	£		£
Investment	20,000		
Loan	10,000		
Total		Total	
Net cash balance *(i.e. Cash In - Cash Out)*			

Answer to Exercise 1.1

Cash in		Cash out	
	£		£
Investment	20,000	Rent	(1,800)
Loan received	10,000	Raw materials	(1,800)
Cash sales	10,500	Salaries	(10,000)
Credit receipts	3,000	Equipment	(16,000)
		Loan payment	(10,000)
Total	43,500	Total	(39,600)
Net cash balance *(i.e. Cash In – Cash Out)*	3,900		

Net cash balance = **£3,900**

So, after six months of trading Melissa's Cupcakes has a cash amount of £3,900 in her bank account. When we say 'net cash balance', it means we are calculating her overall cash position once we take away cash out (the total amount Melissa has spent over six months) from her cash in (the total amount Melissa has sold, savings and loan). So, is her cash position any good? In the next section, we'll have a look at this to get more of an idea.

We can consider Melissa's Cupcakes' cash position as both positive and negative

Positive

1) She started her business just six months ago and has a sum of cash in her bank account ✓

2) She has started to bring in money from her customers ✓

3) She has paid for her equipment upfront, so no longer has this cost to think about ✓

Negative

1) Does she have enough cash to pay for salaries and rent which are due next month? *Maybe*

2) Is there enough left to pay for any emergencies that may arise? *Not much*

3) What about Melissa? She still isn't earning a salary? *Not realistic to continue this way*

4) What if we want to expand our range of cakes, do we have the money to invest? *Not really*

Keep an eye on your cash at all times

CompanyBasix.com

The important point to note is that if Melissa has cash in the bank, then she has the option to pay for things as and when she likes or needs to. So if she wanted to invest more money into testing a new recipe for a cup cake (to generate more sales) she has the cash in the bank to spend on raw materials etc. If her cash position is weak, whereby she is waiting for money to come from her customers, then Melissa may not be able to move quickly and spend freely on testing a new recipe. This is because she does not have the money in the bank to pay for it, and would possibly have to find some temporary cash to keep her going until her customers do eventually pay. The situation is not too dissimilar to a person who is waiting for their salary to come in at the end of the month, but they still have a week to go before it does. They find themselves spending less this week, and may have to borrow money from family or friends if they do not have savings in the bank to keep them going.

What options are available to Melissa to strengthen her cash position?

For the first six months, Melissa's Cupcakes had cash coming in of £43,500 which was a combination of the initial investment (loans and savings) and sales of cupcakes. However, did Melissa need to spend the cash where she did? Could she have done some things differently? Below are examples of where Melissa had no choice in what she did but also where there were opportunities for her to increase her cash position.

- **Rent**: This is usually paid on a monthly basis and unless she has a very generous landlord, Melissa cannot get away without paying this.

- o   Could this have increased her cash position? No.

- **Raw materials**: Payments to suppliers can sometimes be delayed if we enjoy good relations

13

with them. Since Melissa's Cupcakes has only been in business for six months, it's better to pay the bills on time. At this early stage of her business, Melissa doesn't want to create problems with suppliers due to late payments, which may then affect the running of Melissa's Cupcakes.

o   Could this have increased her cash position? No.

- **Salaries**: Again like rent, these need to be paid and Melissa cannot get around this (unless salaries are too high and unsustainable).

o   Could this have increased her cash position? No.

The next two points explain where Melissa has an opportunity to retain more cash in the company bank account.

- **Equipment**: Melissa paid a sizeable sum for the equipment she needed to make her cupcakes. She paid £16,000 in one single payment. The advantages of this are that the company does not need to think about the equipment costs again and it is wise to save paying interest on a loan. However, there are many payment options available to businesses and Melissa could have eased the 'burden' of a tight cash flow by having a financing agreement where she could pay for the equipment over a few years. The estimated useful life of the equipment is 8 years, but if the company paid the full amount over 4 years instead of 1 year, then it would allow her to spread out the payments and help increase the cash available to her in her bank account. Here it is broken down:

Description	Money out
1st year payment	(£4,000)
By paying £4,000 in the 1st year (instead of £16,000 as a single payment), she would pay interest (7%) on the £12,000 outstanding. i.e. £12,000 x 7%	(£840)
Total cash payment	(£4,840)

o Would this have increased her cash position? Yes, Melissa's Cupcakes would have (approx.) an extra **£11,160** in the bank; i.e. Instead of paying out £16,000 in year 1 in one payment, she is paying £4,840. The £11,160 is the difference

• **Loan**: During the year, Melissa paid back £10,000 to friends and family, which was interest free. Could she have agreed to delay paying this back or paid back half, and instead pay interest on this loan? Yes, she could always try doing this, or has the option of applying for a bank loan instead. Let's assume she paid back half of it and agreed with friends and family to pay interest of 10% for the remainder (reasonable to assume this). In this case, she would still be left with more money in the bank than if she had paid the loan back in full:

Description	Balance
Paying half this loan back would mean she still has money in her bank of £5,000	£5,000
If we have this money for another year, at an interest rate of 10%, then we would pay this out	(£500)
Net additional cash in the bank	£4,500

o   Would this have increased her cash position? Yes, by paying half the loan back and paying interest on what she still holds onto, Melissa would have **£4,500** extra left in the bank

For both the equipment and loan, Melissa's company would have paid out approximately £1,340 (£840 [equipment] and £500 [loan]) in interest. Whilst this is not ideal, in the short term, it still amounts to cash in the bank, which is probably more important to Melissa's Cupcakes, as the new business depends on the cash. Melissa now has £15,660 (£11,160+£4,500) extra in the bank than she had before.

There are many other ways Melissa could improve her cash position and these are just a few examples to give you an idea. So in the original scenario Melissa was left with £3,900 in the bank. In this new scenario, when she adds the £15,660, she would have £19,560 in the bank.

For a new business, managing the cash flow is crucial to its survival. Having £19,560 in the bank as opposed to £3,900 would certainly give Melissa the security of knowing she can meet her bill payments - and she also has more money to invest if she chooses to do so.

Summary of the Cash Flow Statement

Just as we need oxygen to breathe, positive cash flow is required to keep businesses going. Without the flow of cash going through a business, it cannot survive. Too many people take their eye off the ball when it comes to managing the money coming in and going out of a business and they only start to monitor cash when they find they don't have the money they need. Well, as important as it is to attract customers to a business, it is even more crucial to ensure a business has the funds to keep going to satisfy and retain these customers. A healthy cash flow builds the foundation for a healthy business.

Cash Flow Statement – Quick-fire questions

1) What are the three main elements of the Cash Flow Statement?

   a) Income, costs and profit

   b) Cash in, cash out and net cash

   c) Assets, liability and equity

2) Cash and profit are the same thing:

   a) True

   b) False

3) Another word for cash is:

   a) Debtors

   b) Creditors

   c) Liquidity

4) Your business may have plenty of customers but it can still be strapped for cash:

   a) True

   b) False

Answers:

1) B: Cash in, cash out and net cash

2) B: False, we will see this more clearly in the next chapter

3) C: Cash is also commonly known in business as liquidity

4) A: True. You may have plenty of customers, but if they all owe you money, then you won't have much cash available to pay off your own creditors. It is a vicious circle when this happens. Stay on top of your cash situation and make sure you have enough money in the bank

Chapter 2

The Profit and Loss Account - *How is my business performing?*

If you can't measure it, you can't improve it – **Peter Drucker**

The Profit & Loss Account is the second of the three main statements we will be looking at in Part 1 of this book. When we want to see how a company is 'performing financially', the Profit and Loss Account is often the main statement that is referred to.

Businesses have a variety of aims and making a profit is probably somewhere near the top. If a company makes a profit, the implication is that it is healthy enough to meet its financial obligations and more. But what is profit and how is it achieved? Profit is simply the difference between the cost of something and the price it is sold at. So if a gadget costs you £2 and you sell it for £3, you have a profit of £1. The Profit and Loss Account tells us how an organisation is making its profit. When I mention the word profit, I could also quite easily mention loss because when we don't achieve one, we get the other.

This diagram shows a Profit and Loss Account in its simplest form.

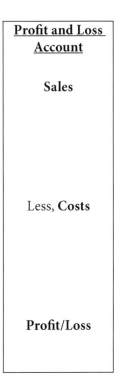

Figure 2.1: Profit and Loss Account

Just like the Cash Flow Statement discussed in Chapter 1, the Profit and Loss Account also has three main sections to it:

- **Sales**: This is what you generate when you sell a product or provide a service.

- **Costs**: The expenses incurred in making the product/providing the service and the operational expenses of keeping the business going.

- **Profit/loss**: This is the 'excess' that is left over when you have taken all your costs away from your total sales.

In this chapter, we'll explore what the Profit and Loss Account consists of and the three elements that go into constructing it. The idea here is to explain the use and workings of the Profit and Loss Account rather than how to construct one; the latter is for accountants to do.

*Income
Revenue
Sales
Turnover*

What's the difference between these four terms?
Answer: Well, they all mean the same thing.

Calculating the sales of a business

In the previous chapter we looked at the Cash Flow Statement, so how does this differ from the Profit and Loss Account? The main difference between the Profit and Loss Account and the Cash Flow Statement is that the latter tracks the movement of cash and explains how we have got to the amount of cash we have in our bank account. The Profit and Loss Account looks at how an organisation is performing in terms of its sales and costs. Many people mistake the two as the same thing, but they certainly are not. Here is an example, highlighting a couple of scenarios where the Profit and Loss Account and Cash Flow Statement differ from each other.

Example 2.1

Matt works for a recruitment company, Recruit with Us, and is a manager in the contracting (temp) division. Cash is important to the company and they want all managers to look after all aspects of the financials, including the cash flow of their own divisions.

Here are two Recruit with Us scenarios:

Scenario 1

In January 20X1, Matt's team generates sales of £115,000, and during the same month his clients have only paid for £100,000. This means some of his clients are going to pay him later. What is the value of his sales: £115,000 or £100,000?

Answer to Scenario 1: The organisation's bank account will show the £100,000 that has been paid. However, the sales generated by Matt's team is still £115,000. So, regardless of how much his clients have paid, his sales are still £115,000.

Scenario 2

Another scenario could be that Matt's team have again generated sales of £115,000 but this time their clients have only paid £5,000. This means there is still £105,000 owed to the company. What is the value of their sales: £115,000 or £5,000?

Answer to Scenario 2: Again, just as scenario 1, the sales figure will be £115,000, even with just £5,000 of the cash having been received.

So for the two scenarios we have just discussed, this is what the Profit and Loss Account and Cash Flow Statement show (we are ignoring Matt's costs for now):

	Profit and Loss Account	**Cash Flow Statement**
Scenario 1	Sales = £115,000	Cash In = £100,000
Scenario 2	Sales = £115,000	Cash In = £5,000

In both of these scenarios, Matt has made sales of £115,000. What is different about each scenario is how much cash he has received. But, regardless of how much cash has been received, he has still made £115,000 in sales.

This explains the difference between the Profit and Loss Account and the Cash Flow Statement. The Cash Flow Statement, as we have discussed, looks at the actual cash in the bank whereas the Profit and Loss Account looks at something else: it looks at performance. The Profit and Loss Account monitors purely the sales Matt's team has generated, regardless of which clients have paid and which have not. So we can see that although in both scenarios sales of £115,000 have been being generated, we only have a healthy cash balance in scenario 1, whereas in scenario 2 we might be struggling to pay our bills.

Loss-making companies can keep going IF they have cash, but profitable businesses without any cash, crash!

Zahoor Bargir

Both the Cash Flow Statement and the Profit and Loss Account give a snapshot of a business' circumstances. The Cash Flow Statement highlights what money has been received by our clients, and the Profit and Loss Account highlights the total sales we have generated from our clients.

To summarise:

- Profit and Loss Account... *looks at* Profit... *which highlights* Performance

- Cash Flow Statement... *looks at* Cash... *which highlights* Survival

Understanding the two main types of costs on a Profit and Loss Account

Now that we've had a look at how sales are classified in a business, let's explore the costs section of the Profit and Loss Account.

Costs (or expenditure) can be divided into two main categories: direct costs and indirect costs. We need to

25

understand these two types of costs because they affect a business' financial performance in different ways, which in turn influences decision-making.

The two main categories of costs in the Profit and Loss Account are:

- Direct costs

- Indirect costs

Direct costs

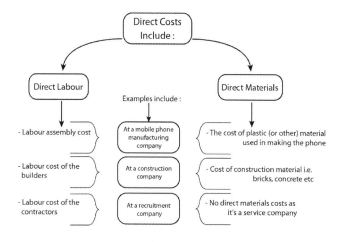

Direct costs can be *directly* attributable to the making of a product or providing a service. If we are a service-based company, like a recruitment company, then direct costs would include labour costs such as the wages of the contractors/temps themselves. Similarly, in a manufacturing context, the direct costs would be related to the making of products such as material and labour costs.

Just like sales can be referred to as revenue, income, turnover, etc., direct costs also have multiple names and are also referred to as cost of sales. An easy way to remember cost of sales is to link it to sales. Any *costs* that you can link directly to *sales* come under cost of sales. For example, if you run a restaurant, you make sales from selling the food on your menu. The direct costs for each menu item are the cost of the ingredients.

Indirect costs

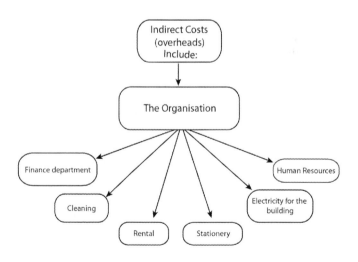

Indirect costs are, therefore, all the other costs that go into the running of the business (or the operation) and which cannot be linked directly to sales or to the making of a product and/or the provision of a service. Examples of this include the salary of the receptionist, rent costs or security expenses etc.

All these expenses, although important to the running of your business, are not involved directly with sales, and so are categorised as indirect costs. Because the receptionist or security is involved in the running of your operation, indirect costs are also known as operational costs or overheads.

Depreciation of assets and indirect costs

Depreciation is a term that's associated with assets that are used over the long term (for more than 12 months) like machinery, fixtures and fittings etc. Depreciation is the decline in price of an asset over a period of time and comes under indirect costs. The asset itself, let's say machinery, might cost £16,000 and may be used for 8 years. In simple terms, this means the asset loses £2,000 each year in value. So in year two the asset is now worth £14,000. This £2,000 reduction in value is seen as an indirect cost.

So the main distinction between the two types of costs is that direct costs (also referred to as cost of sales) are traced directly to the product you make, or the service you deliver, whereas the indirect costs are not.

Exercise 2.1

You are the manufacturer of specialist stools and have the following costs:

Receptionist, factory rent, wood, salesmen's salaries, labourers' salaries, factory insurance, power usage, factory depreciation, steel for stool legs

In the two columns below, allocate these costs as either direct or indirect costs.

Direct	Indirect

Answer 2.1

Direct	Indirect
Wood	Receptionist
Labourers' salary	Factory rent
Steel stool legs	Salesmen's salary
	Factory insurance
	Power usage
	Factory depreciation

So, now I know what direct and indirect costs are, what do they tell me?

Gross and net profit

Just as there are two sets of costs, there are also two bands for profit. These are commonly known as the gross profit and net profit.

The gross profit is what you get when you take away direct costs from your sales. Then when you take away the indirect costs you end up with the net profit. We can incorporate this into the Profit and Loss Account as follows:

	Sales	X
	Less: direct costs	
=	**Gross profit**	X
	Less: indirect costs	
=	**Net profit/loss**	X

So, when we look at these two cost types (direct or indirect), it may seem easier to lump all the costs into one category and see an overall profit. That is one way to see whether you are making a profit or not, but *if you made a loss and wanted to improve the performance of the company, where would you begin to look?*

By knowing the gross profit, you know where to look to improve your company's financial performance; especially if your company is not making a profit. You can find out whether it is the making of a product or the provision of the service that is too expensive or whether you are not charging the right amount, or whether it is the operations side of your company that needs to be looked into, such as overheads or staff costs etc. Whatever needs fixing, the pricing of services or the cost of operations, understanding gross profit provides a starting point of where to focus attention.

Difference between profit and cash

The good news is we're making great profits.
The bad news is you'll be paid in 2 months when we bring in some cash

Since the Profit and Loss Account and the Cash Flow Statements look at different things, it should therefore come as little surprise that there is a difference between profit and cash. One of the main differences between the Profit and Loss Account and Cash Flow Statement is that the Profit and Loss Account shows like-for-like sales and costs during a specific timeframe. The Cash Flow Statement just records the cash coming in and the cash going out as it happens - in real time.

This is another area where many people and business owners take their eye off the ball. We think that because we are building our customer base and focusing on making a profit, we will stay in business. This isn't necessarily true. Profitable companies can fail, just like companies with a good cash flow can fail. It is companies which are profitable AND have sufficient cash at their disposal that have the best chance of being successful.

A business must be able to calculate whether it has been worthwhile spending its resources to generate the volume of sales it has. It's important to see a like-for-like comparison. And we use *time* as the measurement tool to show the sales for a particular month and how they correlate with the costs for that same month. If it looks like the sales generated for the month are less than the costs we have incurred in that month (basically, making a loss), then the business will find it difficult to sustain itself in the long term.

Example 2.2

I have moved into my new business premises and the landlord has requested I pay my rent for six months upfront, at a total cost of £1,800.

What does this look like as a 'cost' item in the Profit and Loss Account and what does it look like as a 'cash out' item in the Cash Flow Statement at the end of the first month?

End of month 1		**End of month 1**	
In the **Profit and Loss Account**		In the **Cash Flow Statement** (or bank account)	
Sales	0	Cash in	0
Costs - rent	£300	Cash out	£1,800

The example shows that the cost of one month's rent will be inserted in the Profit and Loss Account - this is £300 which is one-sixth of the £1,800 we have paid up-front. So although we have paid for six months in advance, we will only show the equivalent of one month's cost in the Profit and Loss Account. In our Cash Flow Statement, however, we show the full amount of £1,800 coming out as this is what has actually left our bank account.

So the difference in what the Profit and Loss Account records and what the Cash Flow Statement records can be summarised as:

Profit and Loss Account	= manual scoresheet.
Cash Flow Statement	= your bank account. Actual money coming in and going out

Summary

No matter what an organisation does, these are the three sections that the organisation's Profit and Loss Account will follow. Charities are different as they don't declare a 'profit' as such. However, they still have income and costs and they call their Profit and Loss Account a Statement of Financial Activities. The major difference is that they don't call it a profit, but instead they call it either a surplus/deficit or 'excess of income over expenditure', or something similar.

If you can remember this format for the Profit and Loss Account, then everything else just follows from here.

Earlier in the Cash Flow Statement chapter we calculated the cash position for Melissa's Cupcakes. This time, we are going to look at Melissa's Profit and Loss Account. Instead of having this as an activity for you, we're going to go through the question together.

The key to each of these items is to take into account only those items that are relevant to business performance.

Exercise 2.2

Melissa's Cupcakes - Calculating the profit for the end of the month

Just like Exercise 1.1 in Chapter 1, listed below are the transactions that have occurred during the six months.

You have already calculated the cash flow in the previous chapter. Now we will go over the profit made during the month of January from the transactions listed below. Under each transaction, I have inserted a note in square brackets as guidance. The numbers in round brackets indicate where to find the entry on the Profit and Loss Account. As you go through each transaction item, put the answer into the Profit and Loss Account template on the next page.

List of all paid and unpaid transactions at end of Dec 20X1	
	£
Cash generated from shop sales of cupcakes *[The £10,500 goes against sales in the Profit and Loss Account] (1)*	10,500
Additional sales of £4,000 made from corporate customers. Of this amount, £3,000 is paid, and £1,000 is still owing *[Regardless of how much cash is received, it is what sales we have generated in this six-month period that is important; which is £4,000] (2)*	4,000
Rent for 12 months *[Because it is six months we are looking at, we only need to consider half this amount. Therefore, £1,800] (3)*	(3,600)
Melissa ordered £2,000 of raw materials. Of this, she paid £1,800. She still owes her suppliers £200 *[Although she ordered the raw materials, it makes no mention of her using any of it to make her product, so leave alone for now]*	(2,000)

Of the raw materials purchased (flour, sugar, cupcake paper cases etc.), Melissa used and sold most of it, and still had about £400 of raw materials left untouched *[She used £1,600 of her raw materials and made sales based on this. This is, therefore, her direct cost] (4)*	(1,600)
She hired 1 full-time staff member at £15,000/year. Melissa has decided not to draw a salary for the first year of business. She also hired 1 part-time staff member at £5,000/year *[Salaries are usually an annual figure, so we need to consider only half this (£10,000). Would salaries be direct or indirect? Let's put it into indirect for now] (5)*	(20,000)
She bought equipment for £16,000 and can use it for 8 years. She paid for this up-front in one payment *[Apportion this cost as depreciation over the asset's useful life – so 1/8 in indirect costs (£2,000); but as this is only for 6 months, we will only apportion half of the year (£1,000)] (6)*	(16,000)
She paid the £10,000 loan back to friends and family *[This has nothing to do with the Profit and Loss Account, because she wasn't charged any interest on this loan from family and friends. We will ignore this for the purposes of this calculation]*	(10,000)

Insert into this table the relevant entries from above

		Dec 20X1
Profit and Loss Account		
Dec 20X1		
	Sales (1) (2)	£
Less direct costs:	Raw materials (4)	£
Gross profit		£
Less indirect costs:	Rent (3)	£
	Salaries (5)	£
	Equip. depreciation (6)	£
Net profit		£

Answer 2.2:

		Dec 20X1
Profit and Loss Account		
Dec 20X1		
		£
	Sales (1) (2)	14,500
Less direct costs:	Raw materials (4)	(1,600)
Gross profit		**12,900**
Less indirect costs:	Rent (3)	(1,800)
	Salaries (5)	(10,000)
	Equip. depreciation (6)	(1,000)
Net profit		**100**

Let's see how Melissa's Cupcakes' profit differs to its cash position

In the Cash Flow Statement chapter, Melissa's Cupcakes had a cash balance of £3,900. Here the Profit and Loss Account tells us that the business has made a profit of £100.

Let's look at this from two perspectives: one looks at Melissa's sales and the cash coming in; the other looks at her costs and the payments going out.

Perspective 1 – Melissa's Cupcakes sales and the cash coming in

Sales in the Profit and Loss Account	£	Cash Flow Statement (cash coming in)	£
Cash sales	10,500	Cash-over-the-counter	10,500
Corporate sales	4,000	Cash received from corporate customers	3,000
		Investment cash	20,000
		Loan money received	10,000
Total sales in the Profit and Loss Account	**14,500**	**Total cash coming in**	**43,500**

We can see there is a difference between sales and the cash flow. Although during this period of time sales of £4,000 were made from corporate customers, Melissa has so far received payment of £3,000 from them, with £1,000 outstanding.

In addition, Melissa's Cupcakes has got in the bank £20,000 of the initial investment and £10,000 received as a loan. Neither of these qualify as sales as both eventually need to be paid back. However, it still counts as cash that has been received in the six-month period.

Similar differences can also be seen in the costs. I have grouped together the direct and indirect costs in the appropriate places below.

Perspective 2 – Melissa's Cupcakes costs and the cash going out

Costs in the Profit and Loss Account	£	Cash Flow Statement (cash paid out)	£
Raw materials	(1,600)	Raw materials	(1,800)
Rent	(1,800)	Rent	(1,800)
Salaries	(10,000)	Salary	(10,000)
Equipment depreciation	(1,000)	Equipment	(16,000)
		Loan payment	(10,000)
Total costs in the Profit and Loss Account	(14,400)	Total cash paid out	(39,600)

Looking at the costs in our Profit and Loss Account, we can see these come in at £14,400 whereas the cash paid out by us is £39,600. This is because of three elements:

1) **Raw materials** - we only show in the Profit and Loss Account the amount of raw materials we have used to make the cupcakes we have sold. Although Melissa bought £2,000 worth of raw materials, she only used £1,600 worth; £400 is still in storage for future use. Looking at our Cash Flow Statement and the cash going out, she has only paid for £1,800. If she has bought £2,000 worth of raw materials, she then still owes her suppliers £200.

2) **Depreciation of equipment in the Profit and Loss Account** - In the Profit and Loss Account, Melissa only reflects the loss in value of the equipment for the period of six months. However, her Cash Flow Statement shows the full £16,000 coming out of the bank because she paid for this equipment in one lump sum.

3) **Repayment of loan of £10,000 to Melissa's friends and family** - because she was merely paying back her loan, it isn't classified as a cost item in the Profit and Loss Account. Melissa was lucky her friends and family provided her with this loan interest free. In any regular lending arrangement, where she may have got a loan from the bank, she would have had to pay interest. And if she had paid interest, this interest amount would be classified as a cost and shown in the Profit and Loss Account.

So bringing it all together, Melissa's Cupcakes *profit* and *cash* situation looks like the following:

Profit and Loss Account	£	Cash Flow Statement	£
Sales	14,500	Cash in	43,500
Costs	(14,400)	Cash out	(39,600)
Profit	**100**	Net cash balance	**3,900**

Overall we can see that profit and cash are two different aspects of finance. Profit is shown in the Profit and Loss Account and cash is shown in the Cash Flow Statement. And it is feasible to have a situation where Melissa has made a profit but she has no cash in the bank or vice versa.

Often, when we want to evaluate a company's financial performance, we should see both the Profit and Loss Account and the Cash Flow Statement. The Profit and Loss Account shows how the company has performed over a specified period and the Cash Flow Statement shows how the company is able to pay for its debts. The two are like a marriage:

CompanyBasix.com

Like a Marriage. *Profit and Cash* are like a married couple.

They are closely linked and are part of the same family but they focus on different things. Neglect Cash and you are doomed! Neglect Profit and you are in for a bumpy ride. Having the two working together will help your company thrive!

Many business scenarios are no more complex than this and it doesn't differ much from how regular household finances are managed. The best position to try to attain is that of a strong profit and cash position. Ultimately, this will ensure the long-term health of a company and keep it sustainable.

What the Profit and Loss Account looks like with operating profit

	Sales	X
	Less: direct costs	
=	**Gross profit**	X
	Less: indirect costs	
=	**Net profit/loss**	X

Earlier in this chapter we discussed the difference between the gross and net profit. However, it is sometimes the case that companies generate sales from items that fall outside their 'normal business.' So, although a call centre company, for example, earns money through making sales calls, it might decide to take advantage of escalating property prices by selling off a building or some land. If it added this new income from the sale of this building to the normal call centre income, it would end up with an inflated income figure, which would have a knock-on effect on the gross profit. Can we then say this increase in gross profit has been achieved through its normal business? No we can't because it has only made this extra profit through a one-off sale of property.

We show this one-off sale of the building in another section of the Profit and Loss Account. So the profit that has been derived *before* this one-off income is called operating profit. And the reason it is called operating profit is because it looks at the profit generated by the company's normal operations. More specifically, the operating profit is the difference between the gross profit and the indirect costs like administration costs, heating, lighting, rent and rates. These indirect costs are also known as operating costs, so if you want to remember how the operating profit is derived, just remember it is after removing the operating costs. After the operating profit, we then show the item 'Other income' which is the one-off income we have generated from the sale of property etc.

So the Profit and Loss Account changes from this:

	Sales	X
	Less: direct costs	
=	**Gross profit**	X
	Less: indirect costs	
=	**Net profit/loss**	X

And now becomes this:

	Sales	X
	Less: direct costs	
=	**Gross profit**	X
	Less: indirect costs	
=	**Operating profit**	X
	Add: other income	X
	Less: other costs	(X)
=	**Net profit/loss**	X

Figure 2.2: Operating profit

So, as you can see in Figure 2.2, the operating profit is calculated by taking the indirect costs away from the gross profit. What this means is that the net profit is calculated once other income and other costs have been taken into consideration.

And just like the other income section which would highlight one-off income items like property, we may also have other costs to accompany it, which would highlight costs that fell outside our normal business operation. Other costs may include the costs incurred in making the sale of the property.

So in between a company's gross and net profit figures, you would see the operating profit, which highlights the profit from the everyday running of your business. And then after taking into consideration a company's other income and other costs, will come its net profit.

The gross profit percentage and what it shows

The gross profit percentage looks at the gross profit as a percentage compared to the sales. Why might we want to look at it as a percentage? Well, it helps when making comparisons and it all comes down to measurability. If a chocolate manufacturer says 'we have made a GP of £200,000' – what does this really mean? Without a benchmark of some sort, on its own it does not say much. However, if we also know that we made a GP of £300,000 last year, then this £200,000 doesn't look as good anymore but at least we have more of an idea. Calculating a percentage figure shows us something a little bit more and in this respect, the gross profit percentage can be a crucial figure.

The gross profit percentage gives us an idea of how we are doing compared with our competitors in a similar industry. If the gross profit percentage has reduced from one year to the next, what is the reason? Is it because our suppliers have increased their prices or is it because we've had to reduce prices in line with our competitors? Knowing the gross profit percentage will also give us an idea of how efficient we are in being able to absorb our indirect costs. After all, we still have to be able to cover these costs.

The formula for the gross profit percentage is:

$$\text{Gross profit \%} = \frac{\text{Sales} - \text{Cost of sales}}{\text{Sales}} \times 100$$

So if a chocolate manufacturer (Choc Company A) made sales of £500,000 with cost of sales (materials and labour) of £300,000, then our gross profit percentage (GP%) would be as follows:

$$\text{Gross profit \%} = \frac{£500,000 - £300,000}{£500,000} \times 100 = 40\%$$

We can see that a gross profit of £200,000 (after sales of £500,000) for this chocolate manufacturer achieves a gross profit percentage of 40%, which is generally a healthy profit margin in most industries. To get an even better idea of whether 40% is good or not, we can compare this to the gross profit percentage of a direct competitor

| | Choc Company A | | Choc Company B | |
	£		£	
Sales	500,000	100%	500,000	100%
Less: cost of sales	(300,000)	60%	(250,000)	50%
Gross profit	200,000	40%	250,000	50%

As you can see, both Choc Company A and Choc Company B have the same sales figure, but by virtue of paying more for their cost of sales, Choc Company A's gross profit percentage is coming in at 40% as opposed to 50% for Choc Company B. This highlights where the difference in financial performance is and can indicate where management may want to focus their efforts, if they are not doing so already.

Summary of the Profit and Loss Account

The Profit and Loss Account is one of the three main financial statements that indicates how a company is performing. Moreover, it highlights how a company is performing over a specific timeframe. However, in addition to highlighting historical financial performance, it can also be used to indicate to management where to focus their attention to boost performance. Through its focus on sales and costs, it brings forth all financial elements of an organisation into a single place, with the ultimate aim of seeing how they are performing together.

Profit and Loss Account - Quick-fire questions

1) Operating costs are also known as

    a) Direct costs

    b) Indirect costs

    c) Costs directly related to sales

2) Sales you made, but haven't received cash for increases your:

    a) Cash

    b) Debtors

    c) Creditors

3) Sales minus your direct costs gives your:

    a) Net profit

    b) Profit after tax

    c) Gross profit

4) Which of the following is a direct cost item?

    a) Depreciation

    b) An electricity bill

    c)   Materials used in making a product we sell

5) Operating profit is calculated by:

    a)   Taking away only your direct costs

    b)   Taking away operating costs from gross profit

    c)   Taking away every type of cost

    d)   None of the above

Tammy and John own a company which sells stationery and here is an extract of their finances: cash sales £81,000, credit sales £40,000, cost of goods sold (stock sold) £20,000, rent £6,000, Tammy's salary (full-time in running operations) £35,000:

6) What is the gross profit figure?

    a)   £101,000

    b)   £81,000

    c)   £86,000

7) What is the net profit figure?

    a)   £60,000

    b)   £81,000

    c)   £86,000

Answers:

1) B: Indirect costs

2) B: Cash owed to you from your sales are known as Debtors

3) C: Gross profit = sales – direct costs (or Cost of Sales)

4) C: An item of stock is seen as a direct cost item

5) B: Operating profit is obtained by taking operating costs away from gross profit

6) A

   Calculation:

   Gross Profit: £121,000 - £20,000 (Cost of Goods sold (COGS)) = £101,000

7) A

   Calculation:

   *Net profit: (£81,000 + £40,000) – (£20,000 + £6,000 + £35,000) = £60,000

(Note: figures highlighted within brackets (above) mean they should be calculated as a group, before moving onto the next part of the formula)

Chapter 3

The Balance Sheet - *How much is my business worth?*

*We will reject interesting opportunities rather than over-leverage our balance sheet – **Warren Buffett***

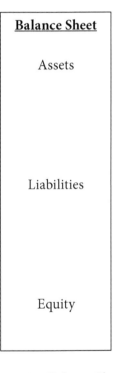

Figure 3.1: Balance Sheet

The Balance Sheet is the third and final part of the three financial statements. It highlights the value of the assets and liabilities of an organisation at any specific time. The Balance Sheet displays the overall health of a company and highlights how much a company is worth. Put simply, and as you can see in Figure 3.1, the Balance Sheet is a list of an organisation's assets and liabilities. So it highlights all that you own and all that you owe.

A Balance Sheet highlights all that you own and all that you owe

Assets

Something valuable belonging to a person or organisation that can be used for the payment of debts

- Cambridge English Dictionary[1]

Assets on the Balance Sheet are a list of all the items that a company owns. They are classified under two sections which are distinguished by the amount of time it takes to convert them into cash:

---

[1] http://dictionary.cambridge.org/dictionary/english/asset

- Fixed assets

- Current assets

Fixed assets

Fixed assets are items organisations own and will hold onto for at least 12 months and are not for resale. These are large items that companies usually need for running the business and include:

- Buildings

- Machinery

- Fixtures and fittings

- IT

- Vehicles

The items mentioned above are likely to stay within the organisation for several years before being replaced. When the term capital expenditure is used, it generally refers to expenditure that has gone on items of a fixed asset nature.

Current assets

These are assets that are more 'liquid' in nature and can be turned into cash very quickly. Such assets include:

- Stock (or inventory)

- Debtors (people who owe us money)

- Bank account/cash

You will have noticed that the bank account is included here. Other items like petty cash (a box in the corner of the office which contains small amounts of cash) may also be consolidated with the bank figure. Each of the items above fluctuate in amount on a monthly (or even daily) basis, hence they are named as current assets. The net cash amount from the Cash Flow Statement is what this bank account/cash figure is.

Any other assets that have not been mentioned would still go in the assets section of the Balance Sheet (above).

Liabilities

A liability is the amount of money that a person or organisation owes

- Cambridge English Dictionary[2]

Just as there are assets a business owns, there are also liabilities that a business owes. And just like the assets, the liabilities come under two distinct categories. These liabilities are also divided by duration, just like the assets. These are:

---

[2] http://dictionary.cambridge.org/dictionary/english/liability

- Short-term liabilities

- Long-term liabilities

Short-term liabilities

These liabilities (also known as current liabilities) are obligations that could change on a month-by-month basis. Or, at the very least, they are obligations that are due to be paid within one year of the balance sheet date. So where we have debtors (people who owe us money) under current assets, we would have creditors (people who we owe money to) under current liabilities. A few short-term liabilities include:

- Creditors (people or organisations we owe money to)

- Short-term loan

- Overdraft

Long-term liabilities

These are costs that a company owes after a year. Such liabilities include:

- Long-term loan

- Mortgage

When we take away the liabilities (both short and long-term) from the assets (both fixed and current), the amount that is left over are our net assets, which is also known as equity.

Equity

Equity highlights the portion of a company the owner owns and this value is calculated by looking at the difference between the assets and liabilities.

$$\left.\begin{array}{l}\underline{\textbf{Assets}} \\ \textbf{Fixed assets} \\ \textbf{Current assets}\end{array}\right\} \quad minus \quad \left\{\begin{array}{l}\underline{\textbf{Liabilities}} \\ \textbf{Short-term Liabilities} \\ \textbf{Long-term Liabilities}\end{array}\right. = \textbf{Equity}$$

Profit and Loss Account balance

The equity section in the Balance Sheet highlights the excess of the total assets over the total liabilities. The example below explains this principle in more detail.

Example 3.1

Imagine Anita buys a house worth £200,000 and gets a mortgage (long-term loan) that is at 90% loan-to value or £180,000. The amount of equity Anita has in the house is, therefore, 10% or £20,000. With house prices rising at a steep rate Anita decides to see what the value of her house is a year later. When she does, she discovers that her house has gone up in value by a whopping £50,000.

Where does that £50,000 go? Well, the mortgage amount remains the same (assuming it is an interest-only mortgage), but it is the equity that Anita has in her house that rises.

So it ends up looking like this:

Balance Sheet

	Original position	**New position**
Assets (house)	£200,000	£200,000
(increase in asset value)		£50,000
Liabilities	(£180,000)	(£180,000)
Equity	£20,000	£70,000

As you can see, the equity amount in the new position has increased by £50,000. So overall, Anita's equity would be £70,000. This is the £20,000 (initial equity) plus the £50,000 (increase in value of the house).

However, what if the house goes down in price? Let's say the house price went down to £170,000 in 12 months' time, from the original £200,000.

	Original position	**New position** (newly-reduced house price)
Assets (house) (reduction in value)	£200,000	£200,000 (£30,000)
Liabilities	(£180,000)	(£180,000)
Equity	£20,000	(£10,000)

So, with the price going down to £170,000, instead of the original equity position of £20,000, Anita would be looking at a negative equity situation where the Equity figure would stand at minus £10,000.

Overall, if the value of the house goes up, it will be a positive for Anita as she gains the benefit of any increase. However, if the value of her house goes down, she will also have to bear this. Anita's liability (long-term) stays the same at £180,000 because this is what the bank has lent her, and obviously, wants this amount paid back (with interest). Whatever Anita's equity in her house, this is what is shown on the Balance Sheet.

In the next section we will be looking at something called working capital, which looks at our assets from a cash perspective.

Net current assets or *Working Capital*

Whether Anita's equity in her house goes up or down, it isn't something that really affects her on a daily basis - so long as she can keep up with her mortgage payments to the bank on a monthly basis. And the same can be said for any organisation. It can own a property and equity works in a similar way to how it would for an individual like Anita. However, whilst their net asset position may not be too much of a concern, it is different when it comes to their net *current* asset position.

Organisations need to consider if they've got the money to pay their creditors and they will also be anxious to receive payments from any parties that owe them money. This way, they can have the money to pay staff salaries etc. To get a better overall picture of a company's funds, take away the current liabilities from the current assets. This helps a company calculate its net current assets, or what is more commonly known as its *working capital*. The name comes from the principle that they are funds (or capital) that are used by a business on a day-to-day basis. Ultimately, the greater a business' current assets in comparison to current liabilities, the more working capital it is deemed to have.

So when a company is looking at working capital, it is looking at items that are pure cash or items that can be converted into cash fairly quickly. Items that can be converted into cash fairly quickly (within days, weeks or a few months) include:

- Items of inventory (or stock) and

- Debtors (organisations that owe us money)

The combined elements of inventory, debtors and cash are, as mentioned earlier, also known as current assets which are available for us to spend on day-to-day operations.

However, this isn't the full picture because organisations also owe money to other organisations. And just like the current assets where this *cash* is available to us fairly quickly, we also have current liabilities where we owe money within a short period of time. And the short period of time mentioned is within one year.

These items that are due for payment within a year (current liabilities) can be offset against the items of cash (current assets) that we have available at our disposal. The difference gives us our working capital.

The formula to remember is:

Working capital = current assets – current liabilities

Why working capital matters

At the heart of any company is working capital, which is a common indicator of a company's overall financial health. It is a measure of how efficient a company is in converting profits into cash and whether it can sustain itself on a daily basis. For small companies it may not be easy to raise funds in the short term, so having a positive working capital position is important to meet bill payments. For larger organisations, a weak working capital position could mean their stock price is affected as shareholders look to sell their shares, and so the value of the shares goes down.

Ways to improve a company's working capital position

If a business finds itself strapped for cash, or wants to shore up its cash position, then there are a variety of ways to do this:

- **Get an overdraft**: One way would be to get a larger overdraft from the bank or secure a long/short-term bank loan of some sort. However, if a business does not require cash urgently at this moment it has other options available to it.

- **Keep a close eye on your debtors' position**: If a business can see that on a month-by-month basis the number of its debtors (customers who owe money) has increased, is this because sales have increased and as a result its debtors have, or is it because the business has been slow in chasing money from its customers? By keeping a close eye on the debtors' position and taking action by speaking with the debtor, it is possible to ensure that payment comes in in a timelier manner.

- **Offer discounts for early payment**: A business could look at improving the number of payments it collects from customers by offering them discounts when they pay early.

- **Reducing stock/inventory levels:** If it looks like a business is holding excess stock, it can look at reducing this so that it only holds stock that is ready for sale or production. This may also require managers to look at their processes to make them more efficient.

- **Renting or leasing fixed assets:** This doesn't form part of the working capital equation, but paying for it certainly does. Can management look at its buying policy for capital expenditure, and instead of buying their own equipment or vehicles, maybe lease or rent the items instead?

This highlights that whilst working capital can give us a good generic picture of the financial position of a business, it should only be used as an indicator. I like to think of working capital as being the heart of a business. If we neglect this, then the whole system fails because the current assets and current liabilities are where you can control a company's cash.

How the Balance Sheet works with the Profit and Loss Account and Cash Flow Statement

The Balance sheet is where the Profit and Loss Account and Cash Flow Statement both come together. When I say 'come together' I mean the net balances of both these statements move into the Balance Sheet to give an overall picture of the business.

Example 3.2

Matt works for a recruitment company Recruit with Us and is a manager of their Contracting (temps) division. Cash is very important to the company and they want managers to look after all the financials, including the cash flow, of their own divisions.

Here are two scenarios:

Scenario 1

In January 20X1, Matt's team generates sales of £115,000 and in the same month his clients have only paid for £100,000 of these sales, which means some of his clients are going to pay him later. What is the value of his sales - £115,000 or £100,000?

The bank account will show that his clients have paid £100,000. However, the sales of his team will still be for £115,000. So, regardless of how much his clients have paid, his sales will still show as £115,000.

Let's take the previous example from Chapter 2 of Matt and his company Recruit with Us. His team generated £115,000 in sales and received £5,000 from their clients. So we summarise it like this:

	Profit and Loss Account	**Cash Flow Statement**
Scenario 1	Sales = £115,000	Cash in = £100,000
Scenario 2	Sales = £115,000	Cash in = £5,000

What we haven't taken into consideration in both these scenarios is what happens to the £15,000 difference between the Cash Flow Statement and Profit and Loss Account in scenario 1 and the £110,000 difference in scenario 2. Well, the difference goes into the Balance Sheet. And because it is money that is owed, it would be shown as debtors in the Assets section (Figure 3.2).

	Profit and Loss Account	**Cash Flow Statement**	**Balance Sheet**
Scenario 1	Sales: £115,000	Cash in: £100,000	Debtors: £5,000
Scenario 2	Sales: £115,000	Cash in: £5,000	Debtors: £110,000

Figure 3.2: Debtors in Current Assets

Conversely, costs which are incurred are shown in the Profit and Loss Account, while what is actually paid for is shown coming out of the Cash Flow Statement. If costs haven't been paid for fully, where do you think the remaining outstanding balance goes? Clue: The previous example showed sales not yet paid going into the assets section. Well, this one is the opposite. So if you guessed the liabilities section in the Balance Sheet you are spot on.

Let's say Matt's company buys stationery for £500 and pays £400 in scenario 1, and in scenario 2, they buy the same amount of stationery of £500 but this time pay nothing at all (Figure 3.3).

	Profit and Loss Account	**Cash Flow Statement**	**Balance Sheet**
Scenario 1	Stationery: £500	Cash out: £400	Creditors: £100
Scenario 2	Stationery: £500	Cash out: £0	Creditors: £500

Figure 3.3: Creditors

The distinction between each scenario, in Figure 3.3, is that in Scenario 2 we have got £500 outstanding which Recruit with Us owes its creditors and in scenario 1 they only owe £100. And because it is for an item that is due in the short-term (within 12 months), it is a current liability. Do note that in either scenario, the Profit and Loss Account still shows £500 as a cost item.

Melissa's Cupcakes and the Balance Sheet for the six months to 31 Dec 20X1

I'm now going to highlight how various items will impact on the Balance Sheet, and also show what else is happening in the Profit and Loss Account and Cash Flow Statement. For ease, I have included a narrative explaining what is happening below the box. The number in brackets is for you to see where it goes in the Balance Sheet, at the end of these examples (Figure 3.4).

- Melissa has opened a cupcake stall called Melissa's Cupcakes on 1st July 20X1 and has invested £20,000 of her own money into it.

	Profit and Loss Account	Balance Sheet	Cash Flow Statement
	£	£	£
Equity *(1)*		20,000	
Cash received from initial investment			20,000

She will have this amount as her initial business capital which goes in Equity and the cash received will be shown in the Cash Flow Statement.

- She had made corporate sales of £1,000 and this money was still owed to her by these customers.

	Profit and Loss Account	Balance Sheet	Cash Flow Statement
	£	£	£
Debtors *(2)*		1,000	
Sales	1,000		

£1,000 is shown in the Balance Sheet because this amount is owed by the customer. And because the customer owes this money, it will be shown as a debtor. The corresponding entry for the £1,000 is also shown in the sales of the Profit and Loss Account.

- Cost of her raw materials (flour, sugar, cupcake paper cases etc.) for the cakes amounted to £2,000. She still had £400 of raw materials left untouched

- Of the £2,000 of raw materials that she ordered, she paid £1,800, leaving £200 that she owed her suppliers

	Profit and Loss Account	Balance Sheet	Cash Flow Statement
	£	£	£
Current assets - stock (3)		400	
Current liabilities – creditors (4)		(200)	

Melissa's Cupcakes has £400 of stock remaining, and this is shown in the Balance Sheet under current assets. It also shows that Melissa owed £200 to her suppliers so this will be shown as creditors, under current liabilities.

- She bought equipment for £16,000 and can use it for 8 years. She paid for this in one single payment

	Profit and Loss Account	Balance Sheet	Cash Flow Statement
	£	£	£
Fixed assets - equipment (5)		16,000	
Cash out			(16,000)

Melissa bought equipment for her business which is shown in the Balance Sheet as a company asset; it will be shown in fixed assets. She also paid for this equipment in one go, so this is reflected in the Cash Flow Statement as money going out.

- Depreciation is 8 years

	Profit and Loss Account	Balance Sheet	Cash Flow Statement
	£	£	£
Fixed assets - equipment (6)		1,000	
Cash out	(1,000)		

Depreciation is the reduction in value of the asset. So over the course of the year the equipment that was bought by Melissa's Cupcakes will reduce in value. As the equipment is scheduled to be used for 8 years, it means the £16,000 (cost of the asset) will reduce over this period, which amounts to £2,000/year. However, because we are only doing accounts for the first six months, the asset has reduced by half of this amount, to £1,000. It is also shown as a cost item in the Profit and Loss Account.

We will put all the Balance Sheet items together into their respective sections and there are two columns of numbers: one column is for the detailed items and figures in the second column are the totals of each section. This is what it ends up looking like:

Melissa's Cupcakes	Balance Sheet at 31st Dec 20X1	
	£	£
Fixed assets		
Equipment **(6)**	16,000	
Less: depreciation **(5)**	(1,000)	15,000
Current assets		
Stock **(3)**	400	
Debtors **(2)**	1,000	
Cash in the bank (balance from the Cash Flow Statement)	3,900	5,300
Short-term liabilities		
Creditors **(4)**	(200)	(200)
Long-term liabilities		
	0	
Net assets		**20,100**
Equity		
Initial investment **(1)**	20,000	
Profit and Loss Account	100	
		20,100

Figure 3.4: Melissa's Cupcakes Balance Sheet

Summary of the Balance Sheet

The Balance Sheet is a statement that highlights all that a company owns - its assets and all that it owes - its liabilities. It shows the overall health of the company in that it summarises the profit (or loss) shown in the Profit and Loss Account and the cash shown in the Cash Flow Statement. Whilst the Profit and Loss Account and Cash Flow Statement are usually seen over a set period of time like: a month, a quarter or a year, the Balance Sheet shows a snapshot of assets and liabilities that a company has over the short and long-term. So the Balance Sheet isn't constrained by time, and is, therefore, often relied upon to give a more complete picture of the financial situation of a company.

Balance sheet - Quick-fire questions

1) Which of these is NOT an asset on the Balance Sheet?

   a) Debtors

   b) Cash in the bank

   c) Loan from S Peters

2) Which of the following is NOT a liability on the Balance Sheet?

   a) Cash in the bank

   b) Creditors

   c) Overdraft

3) Which of these calculations is correct?

   a) Asset – liability = income

   b) Asset – liability = equity

   c) Asset – liability = debtors

4) The Balance Sheet looks at a company's:

   a) Performance

b) Survival

c) Worth

5) Below is a list of your assets and liabilities. When one is taken away from the other, what is the correct equity amount?

Assets: buildings £20,000, debtors £5,000, cash £2,000

Liabilities: creditors £6,000, tax £4,000, bank loan £5,000

a) £12,000

b) £18,000

c) £22,000

6) Karen made sales of £10 and has so far received payment of £8. Where does the remaining £2 go?

a) Cash

b) Debtors

c) Creditors

7) Working capital is calculated by:

a) Current assets - current liabilities

b) Total assets - total liabilities

c) None of the above

8) Working capital matters because:

a) It helps us to become profitable

b) We need it to increase our margins

c) It is a useful indicator of whether we can meet our current liabilities

Answers:

1) C: A loan is a liability

2) A: Cash in the bank is an asset

3) B: Asset – liability = equity

4) C: A Balance Sheet looks at a company's worth. It highlights everything it owns, and everything it owes

5) A

   Calculation:

   Equity is [£20,000 + £5,000 + £2,000] – [£6,000 + £4,000 + £5,000] = £12,000

6) B: The remaining £2 owed to us is classified as a debtor

7) A: Current assets – current liabilities

8) C: Working capital indicates to us how much cash we have to work with within the business, and can therefore, help us ascertain whether we have enough liquidity (cash) to meet our immediate current liabilities and other everyday operational expenses

Part 2

Other elements of the
basic fundamentals

Chapter 4

Fixed and variable costs – *What are the different types of costs?*

*Control your expenses better than your competition. This is where you can always find the competitive edge – **Sam Walton***

In Part 1 of this book, we looked at the three financial statements that highlight the financial position of a company. Part 2 looks at other aspects of a company's financials that link directly to the three financial statements. In this chapter, we will look at two further types of costs that help break down costs in a more meaningful way.

In addition to direct and indirect costs that form different sections of the Profit and Loss Account, a company's costs can be broken down into a further two cost categories:

- Fixed costs – costs that remain the same regardless of how many items we produce

- Variable costs – costs that are affected as and when output changes

Example 4.1

Fixed costs

Imagine you live on your own and have a rental contract for an apartment of £1000/month. For the duration of your rental contract you have to pay this amount each month regardless of whether you are there or not (see Figure 4.1). So even if you go on vacation for three weeks, you still have this fixed cost, called rent, to pay. It does not change.

Fixed cost item

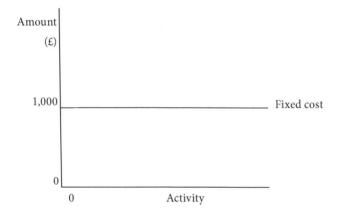

Figure 4.1: Fixed cost line

With variable costs (Figure 4.2), however, this is not the case. If you were to go on holiday for three weeks, then your rent may stay the same (as it is fixed) but your variable costs would change. Take electricity, for example, if you are on vacation, then you can be sure that your electricity bills will change – they will most likely come in lower as the electric isn't being used as much as when you are there. This cost for electric comes under variable costs as it varies with usage.

Variable cost item

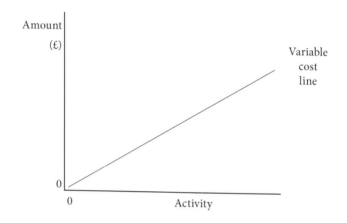

Figure 4.2: Variable cost line

Examples of fixed and variable costs

Fixed costs	Variable costs
Rent	Materials
Salary	Salary (temping costs)
	Electricity
	Heating

Sometimes, fixed costs do change. For example, when you have outgrown where you are based. If you have been renting a warehouse to store your stock, you may find you need a larger warehouse as your business grows and the number of items you have in stock increases.

Figure 4.3 shows how the overall fixed costs line would look if you moved your stock to another warehouse where the rent was more expensive

Stepped Fixed Cost

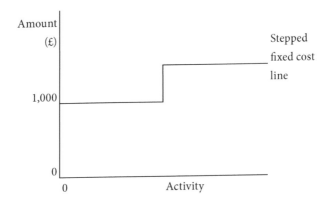

Figure 4.3: Stepped fixed cost

So instead of having a fixed line which goes horizontally, straight across, you may have one which looks more like a step. However, once you have moved into the larger warehouse, the cost of the warehouse will remain constant – and, therefore, fixed.

There are also costs which are a combination of the two types of fixed and variable costs. Such costs, such as a phone bill, might have a fixed element to them (the monthly charge) and then there could be the additional per minute charge which is levied on top. This combination is called 'semi-variable' and is shown in Figure 4.4.

Semi-variable cost

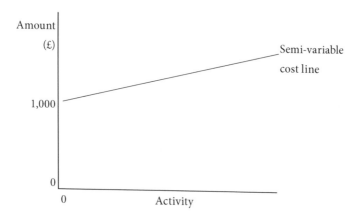

Figure 4.4: Semi-variable cost line

Overall, it's useful to know the shape certain costs take as they can certainly help you to understand what your true costs are and how to account for them.

Break-even point

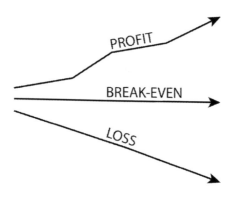

Making a profit is wonderful news and serves to give everyone who is associated with it a welcome lift. Besides making a profit, however, there is another time in business when a certain euphoria is felt that makes all the hard work seem worthwhile. This point in the company's life cycle is called the break-even point. Break-even is desirable as it is one of the first milestones a new company or project goes through which works as an indicator of how you are performing. As well as the financial consideration, there's also the psychological lift one gets when this *tipping point* has been reached.

The **break-even point** is when things are running at **neither a profit, nor loss.**

The break-even point is the point at which things are running at *neither* a profit, nor a loss. It's the point of sales volume where your income (sales) match your expenses and where you are just about making ends meet. The break-even point can be relevant to a project or a company. Because of this, a specific project can be seen as breaking even because its income makes up for its expenditure, but overall, the company may still be making losses because it has other projects that are loss-making.

Knowing your break-even point also enables you to think about what your overall costs are. You may think that you have a sound business idea, but do you have a handle on what your business is actually costing you? And how long are you prepared to keep your business running if you are not generating enough from sales for it to be self-sustaining?

Calculating the break-even point

To calculate the break-even point in terms of sales volume, you need to know the value of three elements:

- Fixed costs - as already discussed, the fixed costs do not change, regardless of how your business is doing. The only way these fixed costs can be recouped is through the excess of the sales price and the cost price of the product.

- Variable costs (of each unit) - the variable cost of producing each product includes things like: material costs, cost of assembly etc.

- Sales price (of each unit) - the sales price of each product you are selling

If you take away the variable cost of each product from the sales price, this leaves you with what is called the *contribution*. The contribution is the amount left over (per unit) that contributes towards the payment of the fixed costs. The reason it is called a 'contribution' as opposed to a profit is due to us not yet having paid for all our costs; we still have our fixed costs to pay. Once the fixed costs have been paid, we can *then* say that we are in profit-making territory.

Example 4.2

Zara's orangeade mini-stall

Zara sets up an orangeade mini-stall at the local community centre and is selling orangeade for £0.20 per cup. The cost breakdown for each cup (or her variable costs) are as follows:

£0.02 per plastic cup
£0.05 orange cordial
£0.03 fizzy water

Total variable costs = £0.10 or 10p

Because it is a community centre, they only charge a notional fixed rent of £5/month.

This means that for every cup of orangeade that she sells, £0.10 goes towards paying for the variable costs, with the other £0.10 'contributing' towards the fixed costs. Fixed costs in this case are rent at £5/month. Once the rent has been covered, Zara is making a profit of £0.10 for every cup she sells.

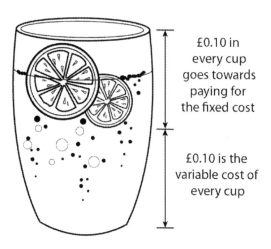

£0.10 in
every cup
goes towards
paying for
the fixed cost

£0.10 is the
variable cost of
every cup

So what is the amount we need to sell to meet our fixed costs? As mentioned, fixed costs in this example consist of rent of £5 per month. If you wanted, it would also be easy to calculate the break-even point for the year by putting in the yearly figure instead of this monthly figure.

The break-even formula is:
Break-even point =   fixed costs ÷ contribution
Break-even point =   £5 ÷ £0.10
Break-even point =   50 cups per month

I can check this another way to see if this is correct:

50 cups   x   contribution £0.10   =   £5 (Rent)

To sum up, Zara needs to sell 50 cups per month to cover the rent of £5, after which she is then making a profit.

Exercise 4.1

What is the break-even point when the company covers its costs in number of units?

A company sells widgets and has two employees. The owner wants to know what her business' monthly costs are and what the break-even point is. Here is a breakdown of the costs:

Rent (including utility costs):	£1000 per month
Fixed monthly salaries:	person 1: £1200 per month
	person 2: £800 per month
Widget materials:	£6 per widget
Sales price of widget:	£16 per widget

Exercise 4.1: Using the information given above, please answer the following questions:

Q: What are the total fixed costs for this widget-selling company, per month?

Q: What are the variable costs per unit (widget)?

Q: Using the formula below, what is the contribution per widget?

Contribution = sales price (per widget) - variable cost (per widget)

Contribution =

Q: Finally, how many widgets do they need to sell to breakeven?

Break-even point   = $\dfrac{\text{monthly fixed cost}}{\text{contribution (per widget)}}$

Break-even point   =

Remember, the break-even point can be calculated on a daily, weekly, monthly, quarterly or annual basis.

Answer 4.1:

Total Fixed costs = £3,000
(i.e. £1,000 (rent) + £1,200 (person 1) + £800 (person 2))

Variable costs per unit = £6 per widget
(in this question, the variable costs have been combined into one figure)

Contribution per unit = £10
(i.e. £16 - £6)

Break-even point = **300 units**
(i.e. £3,000 ÷ £10)

So what the business has discovered is that it needs to sell 300 units of these widgets to be able to cover both its fixed costs and variable costs (its total cost). As a check, another way to see how this can be calculated is as follows:

Variable costs	+	fixed costs
£1,800	+	£3,000
(i.e. £6 x 300 units)		
Total cost	=	£4,800

Another check		
Breakeven	x	sales price
300 units	x	£16
Total cost	=	£4,800

Limitations of the break-even calculation

Like any tool, there will be some limitations which include:

- Due to its simplicity, it is more useful for individual projects than for an organisation that may have multiple products in its portfolio.

- Many products have a combination of fixed and variable costs related to them and so it is not always easy to associate specific costs to a product.

- Although it is a useful indicator of what we have to achieve to be able to meet our costs, it doesn't give us much information on what demand for the product is like out there.

Summary of different types of costs

Keeping a handle on the various types of costs within a business can help track the various liabilities affecting a business. The break-even analysis is a useful tool for making decisions and helps you understand the nature of the various types of costs you have. In this increasingly competitive commercial world, knowing how your costs impact the Profit and Loss Account means you can make quick decisions to favourably impact your profitability and cash flow.

Fixed and variable costs - Quick-fire questions

1) The contribution per unit is calculated by:

   a) Sales price – fixed cost

   b) Sales price – variable cost

   c) Fixed cost – variable cost

2) The break-even point in units is derived from:

   a) Fixed costs ÷ contribution per unit

   b) Fixed costs ÷ variable cost per unit

   c) Fixed costs ÷ sales price per unit

3) Which of these costs would come in lower if total units of production came in below what was originally budgeted?

   a) Total fixed costs

   b) Total variable costs

4) A business makes widgets and spends £34,000 on materials and also £36,000 for manufacturing staff at current production levels of 2,500 units. Head office costs (inc. staff) are £100,000. To achieve break-even, the selling price per unit would have to be:

a) £68

b) £84

c) £96

5) Instead of 2,500 units, it has been assessed that production levels will need to change to 2,000 units instead. To achieve break-even, will the selling price per unit, therefore, have to:

a) Decrease

b) Increase

c) Remain the same

6) How much would the new selling price be at the new production level of 2,000 units:

a) £113

b) £98

c) £78

Answers:

1) B: Sales price – variable cost

2) A: Fixed costs ÷ contribution per unit

3) B: Total variable costs. Your fixed costs would just stay the same regardless of the level of output

4) A: £68
   Calculation:

   Variable costs   = £28
   (i.e. (£34,000 + £36,000) ÷ 2,500 units)

   Contribution   = £40
   (i.e. £68 - £28)

   Break-even point = 2,500 units
   (i.e. £100,000 ÷ £40)

   Sales price   = £68

5) B: Increase the sales price because a smaller number of units (2,000) need to make up for fixed costs of £100,000, where before you had 2,500 units to help cover this cost.

6) C: £78

Calculation:

Contribution   = £50
(i.e. £100,000 (fixed costs) ÷ 2,000 units

New sales price = £78
(i.e. £50 + £28 (variable costs))

Chapter 5

Invoicing and accruals – *When to record income and expenses*

Being in control of your finances is a great stress reliever - **Anonymous**

Businesses that flourish use accurate financial information because it helps their leaders to make accurate and timely decisions. Monthly profit figures in the Profit and Loss Account consist of sales and costs that have occurred in the same month. So income, direct costs and indirect costs in the Profit and Loss Account need to cover the same timespan (month, quarter or year) to provide a true figure of financial performance.

However, what if we pay direct costs (like salaries) in one month but don't actually invoice for the sales generated until the following month? Does this mean we don't record any sales in that month? Absolutely not! It just means we have not invoiced for the sales, even though a sale was actually made. So what is an invoice and how does it work?

The concept of invoicing

An invoice (sometimes called a bill) is a legal document (usually just a single page) that is produced by the seller and sent to the buyer for the sale or provision of a product or service. It states the description of the goods/services provided, the quantity and the sale price. It will also have other details like the seller's address as well as who the buyer is.

Often, it is referred to as a sales invoice (if you are the seller), or the purchase invoice (if you are the buyer). Either way, the invoice is only generated by the seller.

When is the Invoice generated?

For either a product or service, an invoice can be generated:

- **Product**: As soon as the product has left the seller's warehouse and is on its way to the buyer.

- **Service**: When a service has been fully provided. So when a plumber completes the job of fixing a leak, they can then raise an invoice to give to the client.

Example 5.1

You sell printer cartridges and an order has been made from a customer for 10 cartridges at £20 each. It is currently 30th April and the cartridges will leave your warehouse on 2nd May.

As the seller, when can you raise an invoice for £200 – 30th April or 2nd May?

Answer: 2nd May

However, someone may ask the question: The order was made on 30th April, can't the sale be shown in April even if we can't raise an invoice until 2nd May?

Answer: No.

In the example above, the cartridges were sent to the customer on 2nd May, so the customer is only obliged to pay you as of that date. Before this date, the customer can always change their mind.

Example 5.2

Following on from Example 5.1, the customer has made the order on 30th April and you send the cartridges out on 30th April (the same day). However, you will raise a sales invoice on 2nd May (the Finance department are slightly behind with the raising of the invoice), can we now show the sale in April?

Answer: Yes.

You can now show the sale happening in April as the goods were sent off in April. And you can show this sale by way of raising an 'accrual' (more on this term a little later), because the invoice was raised the following month, in May.

Example 5.3

Allia has started her own affordable jewellery company called Maglace, which specialises in magnetic necklaces. She has started to distribute her jewellery to one outlet, Jan's

Jewellers, who like her creations and have bought in bulk. She started trading in January 20X1. Below are two columns: one for January 20X1, and the other for February 20X1. Here is a list of her individual sales and cost items for the month.

Sales:

Maglace received an order of £1,400 for jewellery from a customer on 28th January, and sent it via courier to the customer on the same day. Maglace then raised and posted the sales invoice to the customer on 3rd February (Figure 5.1). In the financials it will look like this:

	Jan 20X1	**Feb 20X1**
	£	**£**
Sales		1,400

Figure 5.1: Sales

The reason the sale is shown in the February accounts is because this is when the invoice was raised. If the invoice had been raised in January and sent with the jewellery, then the £1,400 sale would be shown in January instead.

Someone may ask the question: Can't I just change the date of the invoice to January 15, and post it in the previous month's accounts?

Answer: Well, in accounting, when a set of figures have been finalised for the month, it stays this way and the numbers do not change. We call this a 'month-end close'. This is to maintain the integrity of the numbers, otherwise, you'll have a set of figures that keep changing and the numbers will have no credence. So, once a month is said to have been 'closed', we can no longer post into that period.

Costs:

Maglace ordered and received £600 worth of materials to make jewellery in January (Figure 5.2). The company received the purchase invoice for the jewellery in January, so the cost will be shown in January.

	Jan 20X1	Feb 20X1
	£	£
Sales		1,400
Less:		
Direct costs: materials	(600)	

Figure 5.2: Direct cost - materials

In the month of January, Maglace also received a purchase invoice of £200 for marketing (Figure 5.3). This cost for marketing will also be shown in January.

	Jan 20X1	Feb 20X1
	£	£
Sales		1,400
Less:		
Direct costs: materials	(600)	
Indirect costs:		
Marketing	(200)	

Figure 5.3: Indirect cost - marketing

Maglace's phone usage in January was £60, and she received the purchase invoice for this in February (Figure 5.4). In this instance, because she received the invoice in February, the cost will be shown in the accounts in February.

	Jan 20X1	Feb 20X1
	£	£
Sales		1,400
Less:		
Direct costs: materials	(600)	
Indirect costs:		
Marketing	(200)	
Phone		(60)

Figure 5.4: Indirect cost - phone

Other miscellaneous costs in January amounted to £200 (Figure 5.5). Purchase invoices were received in January, so these costs will be shown in the accounts in January.

	Jan 20X1	Feb 20X1
	£	£
Sales		1,400
Less:		
Direct costs: materials	(600)	
Indirect costs:		
Marketing	(200)	
Phone		(60)
Miscellaneous costs	(200)	
Net profit/(loss)	**(1,000)**	

Figure 5.5: Miscellaneous costs

Looking at the January column, when we take away the direct and indirect costs from the sales, it shows a net loss of £1,000.

Is this correct? Do we really have a net loss of £1000? Actually, we do not have a loss because of a couple of things:

- Maglace made sales in January but it only sent the sales invoice to its customer in February. However, the sale was still made in January as the customer received their jewellery in that month.

- Maglace's phone bill for January has come through the post in February. However, this too is a cost attributed to January, and has to been shown as such.

So the income of £1,400 should be shown in January and the costs were incurred in January of £60 (phone bill) should also be shown in January. They aren't because of timing issues but there is a way of dealing with this to reflect this in the accounts.

The matching concept – dealing with timing issues

In accounting terms there is something called the 'matching concept' which stipulates that income generated must be compared against costs incurred in that same period. This then gives a more accurate account of the profit obtained.

In Maglace's example, therefore, the sale of £1,400 (Figure 5.1) and the cost of the phone bill (Figure 5.4) should be in the January column as they are related to that month (January 20X1). If they were, then the loss of £1,000 would have been different. This is what it should have looked like (Figure 5.6) when these amounts are reflected in January:

	Jan 20X1	Feb 20X1
	£	£
Sales	1,400	
Less:		
Direct costs: materials	(600)	
Indirect costs:		
Marketing	(200)	
Phone	(60)	
Miscellaneous costs	(200)	
Net profit/(loss)	**340**	

Figure 5.6: Correct input in Jan 20X1
of Sales and Phone costs

Therefore, if the income and expenses were shown in the correct month, Allia's company Maglace would have shown a *profit of £340* instead of the *loss of £1,000*. So how can we show the income and costs in the month that they relate to, if we only generate the sales invoice and receive the purchase invoices in the next month?

Well, this is where the concept of the *accrual* comes in.

What is an accrual?

The website *dictionary.com*[3] describes an accrual as 'a charge incurred in one accounting period that has not been paid at the end of it'. So you are technically buying something now and showing in the accounts you have bought it but are paying for it later. However, this only highlights the expenses (or costs) side of it. Conversely, an accrual can also be 'an Income item that has been earned but is yet to be invoiced for.'

An accrual is temporary, but an invoice is permanent

To all intents and purposes, an accrual is just a temporary measure. For income, we will still raise the sales invoice to the customer for the work done. And for costs, we will still process the cost invoice. An accounting system is where

---

3   http://dictionary.reference.com/browse/accrual?s=t

both types of invoices get recorded. However, until invoices actually get processed in the accounting system, we will raise an accrual temporarily in place of the expected invoices in the correct period necessary.

I liken an accrual to a 'ghost-like' item because it comes in and goes out. And just like 'Slimer', the ghost in Ghostbusters that leaves slime wherever it goes, an accrual also leaves a trace. It serves as a 'temporary' sale/cost in place of the missing sale/purchase invoice that we're waiting to send out or arrive. If you have an accountant or finance department then they will be able to physically put the accrual in for you. However, the accrual amount itself should come from you as you will have an idea as to what the approximate cost will be.

Just like two sides of a coin, there are also two sides to an accrual and here is how an accrual actually works:

Side 1 of the accrual

Let's take the Maglace example (Figure 5.4) and use the phone bill of £60 for this exercise.

Allia knows that she has used the phone in January and that this is a cost to the business for that month. However, the actual invoice for this cost (from the supplier) won't come through until the following month, February.

Description		Month
		Jan 20X1
What is the cost that has been incurred?	Phone charge	
Has the invoice for this cost come through?	No	X
We should, therefore, accrue. To accrue we do need an amount to put in. But what if I don't know what the actual cost amount is going to be? In this instance, we should just estimate the amount	Estimate of accrual: £60	£60
Amount of the accrual		£60

Figure 5.7: Accrual input

At the end of January, our Profit and Loss Account will show a phone expense for £60, due to the accrual (Figure 5.7). This is before we have received the actual invoice, which will arrive the following month.

Side 2 of the accrual

Side 2 is all about the opposite of the initial accrual figure. Earlier I mentioned it being a 'ghost-like' item that comes in and goes out; well we are now going to look at it going out. So far, what we have done looks like this:

	Jan 20X1	Feb 20X1
	£	£
Invoice of phone bill	X	60
Accrual in – Jan	60	

Figure 5.8: Accrual coming out in the next month

In January 20X1 we put in an accrual in the accounts of £60 for phone expenses. And on the 15th of February we receive the actual invoice of £60 for this phone expense (See Figure 5.8). So if we process this invoice it will show up in our February 20X1 Profit and Loss Account as a charge of £60. If we have already accounted for this charge in January 20X1 as an accrual and shown it in the February 20X1 Profit and Loss Account as a purchase invoice, is this not putting the cost into the Profit and Loss Account twice?

At this stage our 'ghost-like' item of the accrual of £60 needs to come out, and it does so in February 20X1 for exactly the same amount.

Let me show you how this works:

	Jan (£)	Feb (£)
Phone bill received	X	60
Accrual in – January	60	
Accrual out – February		(60)
Cost shown in January P&L Acc.	60	0

Figure 5.9: Accrual coming out in the next month

Initial accrual of £60 is now coming out: i.e. it is a negative

As you can see, the accrual comes out in February and this is shown as a negative. What this does is offset the invoice amount which is shown in February, as the accounts already show this cost in the previous month (January). By doing this we can see that:

- The phone cost (£60) is shown only once in our accounts as a net amount (see the final line of the above diagram – Figure 5.9).

- We can show the cost in the month that it was incurred – in this case, January.

- We have more control over our costs as we know what has been recorded in the accounting system and what has not. So we know what the accounting system is supposed to show even if we don't have the invoices.

Exercise 5.1

Allia has agreed that she will sell £650 worth of jewellery to a customer and today's date is the 15th of March. The customer receives the jewellery on the 25th of March and Allia has not yet raised the sales invoice.

If we assume Allia will raise the sales invoice in April, what does she put into the accounts in March?

a) Raise a cost accrual for £650

b) Raise a sales accrual for £650

c) None of the above

Answer 5.1: b) Raise a sales accrual for £650. Sales accruals work in exactly the same way as cost accruals.

Summary of invoicing and accruals

Having accurate financial data means decisions can be made quickly and with a high degree of confidence. Being able to match sales generated in a particular time period with costs incurred in that same period is paramount to generating this financial data. Knowing when invoices are recorded in the accounting system helps us to understand when services being procured are being accounted for. And this is where accruals play a crucial part in this process each month. It means that regardless of when supplier invoices come in, costs can still be accounted for because we would accrue for them. Conversely, we can also use accruals to help us track our sales. We can raise an accrual in the period the sale has been made, knowing full well that a sales invoice has not yet been raised.

Accruals - Quick-fire questions

1) An accrual can be related to:

    a) Costs only

    b) Income only

    c) Both income and costs

2) We need to provide for accruals in our accounts because of:

    a) The duality concept

    b) Depreciation

    c) The matching concept

3) A cost accrual is an accounting tool that:

    a) Allocates costs in the correct period in which they were incurred but not paid

    b) Allocates costs in the correct period they were incurred and paid

    c) Allocates costs in the period for which they have yet to be incurred

4) Why does an accrual amount sometimes differ from the actual invoice amount that it relates to?

a) The invoice comes first and so the accrual is then out of date

b) The accrual and the invoice are obviously not related, otherwise they would match

c) An accrual is sometimes only an estimate of the incurred cost. The invoice comes later

Answers

1) C: Accruals can be relevant to income as well as costs

2) C: The matching concept. Income generated for the month should be matched up against the costs incurred in that same period

3) A: An accrual allocates costs in the correct period in which they were incurred but not paid

4) C: An accrual is sometimes only an estimate of the incurred cost. The invoice comes later

Chapter 6

Budgeting – *Keeping a plan*

*A budget is telling your money where to go instead
of wondering where it went –* **Dave Ramsey**

Balancing the books!

Whether it is on a personal level or for a project or business,
budgeting is something we cannot get away from; it helps us
plan financially. And yet for many of us budgeting seems to
be a tricky exercise.

Experts in their particular field can quite easily struggle
with budgets. I was flicking through TV channels the other
day and came across a dishevelled gentleman who looked
rather distressed. It was a cookery programme and I became

curious. Turns out that the gentleman looking distressed was a hotel owner who, along with a panel of judges, was looking for a Head Chef, and thought he'd found the perfect person. Certainly, the plate of food the Head Chef had produced was of the highest quality. However, when the judges asked the Head Chef how much the items on the plate had cost, he could only give a ball-park figure. They were more interested in the financial details of the plate since he would be in charge of buying such items in bulk.

The judges were surprised that someone so good at his craft did not know how much it all cost. And the Head Chef was also quite disappointed with himself as he knew keeping on top of his spend was going to be a large part of his role. Besides, if he did not know how much each plate had cost, how could he know how to price it up? But he knew why his knowledge of the costings was lacking. He had always known that finance was not his strong point, so he avoided it altogether, choosing instead to focus on the cooking, which he knew he was good at.

This need not have happened to the Head Chef and it certainly does not have to happen to you. We have already gone through many of the key financial concepts in this book and in this chapter, I will put together what a budget looks like and describe its basic elements.

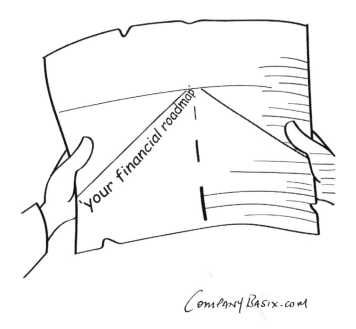

CompanyBasix.com

The main aspects of a budget

- It is financial planning into the future – usually done the year before

- It usually spans 12 months, although a budget can also be made for shorter/longer periods

- A budget can be of the Profit and Loss Account, the Balance sheet and the Cash Flow (although, it is common for most non-financial people to look after a budget of a Profit and Loss Account and Cash Flow)

- It looks at sales and expenses (more common for people to focus on the spend, but budgeting also looks at income)

- It enables us to compare what we projected our performance to be against how we have actually performed

- Keep it simple and remember to keep a record of the notes that underpin where your figures have been generated from, including any assumptions you make. i.e. there is a possibility that the price of raw materials is going to increase so you've reflected this in your budget.

The Budget format

The first column of the budget looks exactly like the Profit and Loss Account, with sales, direct costs and indirect costs. We then have columns which span the next 12 months because this is usually the period into the future that we are looking at. And at the end of these 12 months, there is a 'Total' column which adds these 12 months together to give an overall consolidated picture of the 12 months.

Here is an example of what a format of a budget could look like:

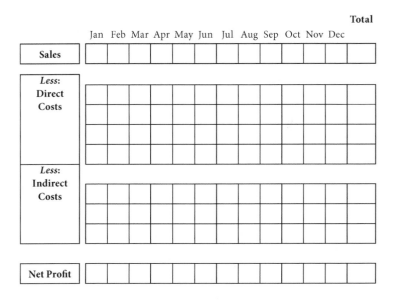

Figure 6.1: budget template

Once these empty 'cells' in Figure 6.1 have been filled in with *your* projected figures, the budget is complete - at least for the Profit and Loss Account. The challenging part is making assumptions in order to estimate what future sales and costs might be. However, this provides a good basis to look closely at your business; to understand the details that will impact on your financial performance.

Once the budget has been agreed and set, it then forms the benchmark against which actual financial performance is measured

Once the budget has been agreed and set, it then forms the benchmark against which the actual financial performance is measured - and this happens during the year.

A budget for the cash flow is exactly the same as that of the Profit and Loss Account, albeit replaced with the Cash Flow Statement sections instead. We will not be looking at doing a Balance forecast as this is usually the domain of an accountant or the finance department. But overall, it follows the same principle of the Profit and Loss Account and Cash Flow Statement, where it is extended over 12 months.

The difference between a budget and a forecast

Most of us have heard of a budget and we may also have heard of a forecast. But what is the difference between the two?

1) A budget is usually created before the start of the year in question and the forecast is done during the year. If you were doing a budget for the year January

20X6 to December 20X6, the budget will usually have been done in 20X5. A forecast gets updated periodically during the year.

2) Forecasting is done 'in-year' because we obviously have more of an idea of how things are turning out during the year, than we did before the year began. Based on this new knowledge we would 're-forecast' to see how the rest of the year is potentially going to turn out.

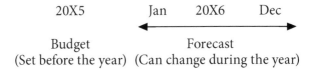

| 20X5 | Jan | 20X6 | Dec |

Budget   Forecast
(Set before the year)   (Can change during the year)

4) A budget stays fixed whereas a forecast is more fluid. A forecast is, therefore, seen as more of an accurate reflection of what is happening in your business than a budget.

5) A budget looks at *where* you want to be, whereas a forecast shows you *how* you are progressing in getting there. The aim is for both to get to the same place, although sometimes this is not the case.

The format of the forecast is just the same as the format for the budget, see Figure 6.1. A cash flow budget highlights when cash will be coming in (i.e. approximately when your customers will be paying you) and when cash is going to go out (i.e. when you will be paying for your expenses). This forecast can highlight possible cash shortages which will focus the mind earlier on how these can be avoided. Seeing a possible 'red light' ahead of time is beneficial as it allows you time to make contingency plans, if needed.

Few organisations, especially start-ups, spend enough time on a cash budget or forecast. It's not enough just to have a Profit and Loss Account budget when it is the cash (or lack of it) that can put you out of business.

A simple cash forecast format might look something like this:

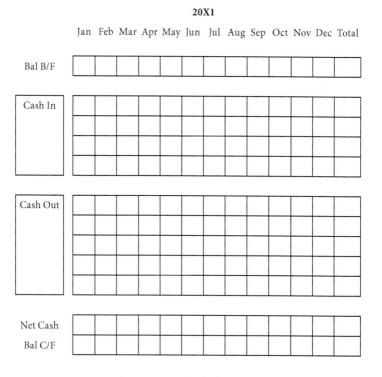

Figure 6.2: Cash forecast

This is a monthly Cash Flow Statement, but I have worked with clients who keep one on a weekly, or even daily, basis.

Exercise 6.1

We discovered in Chapter 1 how Melissa's Cupcakes had £3,900 of cash left for the 6 months ending 31st Dec 20X1. Going forward, she has now forecast that her business will bring in the following cash over the next 6 months:

Cash in:

- £2,500 cash coming in from sales to customers per month (rising by 2% each month from February).

- To ensure she had enough cash for the business, Melissa went back to her family and borrowed £5,000; this money came in 2 equal amounts in January and February.

Cash out:

- Salaries levels were kept the same for the next 6 months. A full time person on £15,000 per annum, and a part-time person on £5,000 per annum. Melissa does not take out a salary. Salaries quoted are inclusive of all insurances and taxes.

- Raw material payments to suppliers are forecast to be £200 per month (rising by 2% each month from February).

- Business insurance is £1,000 for the year, payable in 2 equal instalments – one in January and the other in March.

- Rent is £3,600 per annum and is paid monthly.

Exercise 6.1: In the table below, calculate Melissa's forecasted cash position for the 6 months ending 30th June 20X2

Cashflow forecast 6 months to end Jun 20X2

	Jan	Feb	Mar	Apr	May	Jun
Bal B/F	3,900					
Cash In						
Sales						
Loan						
Cash Out						
Salaries						
Raw materials						
Co. insurance						
Rent						
Net Cash						
Bal C/F	3,900					

Answer to Exercise 6.1

Cashflow forecast 6 months to end Jun 20X2

	Jan	Feb	Mar	Apr	May	Jun
Balance B/F	3,900	6,233	9,113	9,039	9,513	10,036
Cash In						
Sales	2,500	2,550	2,601	2,653	2,706	2,760
Loan	2,500	2,500				
Cash Out						
Salaries	(1,667)	(1,667)	(1,667)	(1,667)	(1,667)	(1,667)
Raw materials	(200)	(204)	(208)	(212)	(216)	(221)
Co. insurance	(500)		(500)			
Rent	(300)	(300)	(300)	(300)	(300)	(300)
Net Cash	2,333	2,879	(74)	474	523	573
Balance C/F	6,233	9,113	9,039	9,513	10,036	10,609

The bank balance at the end of the 6 months is forecasted to show £10,609. Considering £5,000 of this amount is coming in the form of a family loan, the business' cashflow shows only a mild increase on the initial position of £3,900 that was at the beginning of the year. It also highlights the role the loan is playing in giving Melissa's Cupcakes that little bit of a buffer.

Upon closer inspection of the monthly cash position, we can see that in the month of March the Net Cash goes into a negative of £74. This can be important as it highlights a monthly deficit and shows how tight the cash situation can be on a monthly basis. Since we have a cash balance of over £9,000, running a small deficit for one month is not a major concern. For such a small business, it would be advisable to manage the cashflow on a daily basis so that it is better placed to deal with its finances.

The variance – seeing differences

We have discussed the budget and the forecast and their differences, but what's missing is the actual. When we talk about 'actuals', we are looking at what income and costs happened in reality against what we thought would happen (our budget or forecast). Actual results are important because it is the actual that is measured against both the budget and/ or forecast. And whichever numbers the actual results are measured against (whether they are measured against the budgeted figure or the forecasted figure), the difference is known as the variance.

We can show the variance in a simple table (Figure 6.3) that shows the comparison of the actual against the budget.

	Actual	**Budget**	**Variance**
Sales	100	120	(20)

Figure 6.3: Sales variance

The amount (20) in the variance column signifies that our actual income achieved is 20 short of what we had originally budgeted, and is, therefore, a *negative* figure. It is quite common for accountants to use brackets to highlight a negative figure instead of a minus, as a bracket cannot be mistaken for a dash, like a minus figure can. Conversely, the cost variance looks like this in Figure 6.4:

	Actual	**Budget**	**Variance**
Cost	100	120	20

Figure 6.4: Cost variance

Here, the amount of 20 in the variance column is a *positive* figure as we have actually spent less than what we had originally expected to.

Sometimes, a negative variance is also described as an *adverse* variance, and a positive variance is described as a *favourable* variance. It is also quite common for *adverse* variances to be shown in a table in red.

As you can see on the budget format, each month has a profit figure attributed to it. This is because we want to know how we have performed financially on a monthly basis. So it is important to have accurate financials which give us a true picture, and accruals play an important part in this picture.

Summary of budgeting

As the adage goes, if you don't know where you are going, all roads lead to somewhere. To be able to budget and forecast is a tool we not only need in business but in life in general. Every business decision we make has a financial impact and if we can plan ahead how certain things are likely to pan out, then we can make provisions earlier for any eventualities. Whether we have a fixed budget and use a forecast to keep tabs against this budget, or whether we just have a budget on its own, these are ultimately tools to help us. Keep it simple and remember to keep your notes that underpin where your figures have been generated from. You can then use the figures on paper to help you focus on working out how to make a success of your business.

Congratulations on reaching the end of *Unpuzzling Finance*. You have gone through all there is to know about the basics of finance. The terms and methodology I have shared in this book highlight the very foundation of a business' finances and what they mean. By going through this book you have opened up a world that is still quite foreign to many people; one they still find puzzling. Whether you are a business owner or a manager, or looking for a promotion, and whatever field you are in, knowing these basics is a big step towards improving your financial literacy. Just as good food is necessary to sustain a healthy body, improving your financial knowledge will increase the possibility of financial stability for you, your department, your business etc. By sharing this knowledge with thousands of people in my workshops, I've seen how their confidence has grown. It is my hope that you will share these fundamentals with others too.

Budgeting - Quick-fire questions

1) A forecast is the same as a budget?

   a) True

   b) False

2) A budget can only be set for a fixed period of 12 months:

   a) True

   b) False

3) If we forecasted that materials would cost £650 but the actual cost was £850, what is the variance?

   a) £200 positive variance

   b) (£200) adverse variance

   c) (£850) adverse variance

4) If we forecasted that income would be £1,500 but the actual income was £1,700, what is the variance?

   a) £200 positive variance

   b) (£200) adverse variance

   c) (£1,700) adverse variance

5) It was budgeted that income for the month of August was going to be £2,000 but in fact was £1,800. What is the variance for this income?

a) £1,800 favourable variance

b) (£1,800) adverse variance

c) £200 favourable variance

d) (£200) adverse variance

6) Cash forecasts can be updated on a daily basis:

a) True

b) False

Answers:

1) B: False. Budgets are usually set before the year starts, and forecasts are updated during the actual year

2) B: False. A budget can be set for any period of time. It can be set for six months, or even 18 months

3) B: (£200) adverse variance because we spent £200 more than we originally intended

4) A: £200 positive variance because we brought in £200 more than we thought we would

5) D: (200) adverse (2,000 – 1,800). We got £200 less income than we had anticipated

6) A: True. To stay on top of their cash situation, many companies keep a daily record of their cash position, so a daily Cash Flow Statement forecast isn't that unusual

Glossary

Accrual. This is the act of making a provisional record for:

a) Income that has been earned (but your haven't yet sent out the invoice for receiving payment), or

b) Expenses that you have incurred and which you have not yet paid.

For example, if you used your mobile phone in January, then this cost is related to January in your accounts through an accrual. The service provider, however, will send you an expense invoice in February but it is still related to January. Accordingly, an accrual for income works in a similar fashion. If you sell your services by creating websites, and you completed a website in January, then this income is related to the month of January. You may raise and send the invoice to your customer in February, but it is still related to work done in January.

Amortisation. This is similar to depreciation with the main difference being that it is in relation to intangible assets, as opposed to tangible assets. Intangible assets are assets that have value but which cannot be touched. Such items include goodwill or intellectual property. Intellectual property has a value attributed to it, although it does decrease in value over time. This decrease in value is the amortised portion that, just like depreciation, comes out as an expense in the Profit and Loss account.

Balance Sheet. Highlights the value of the assets (current and long-term) and liabilities (current and long-term) of a business at a specific time. In simple terms, it looks at the 'worth' of a company and this is generally the net result of what it owns and what it owes.

It is more common for the Balance Sheet to be drawn up at the end of the month, quarter or year.

The formulae that are relevant for the balance sheet include:

Assets - liabilities = equity   OR   Assets = liabilities + equity

Break-even point. This is the point at which the sales generated and the costs incurred are the same. So this is the moment we are neither making a profit, nor a loss. It is a useful psychological measure that shows how well you are doing, especially in the early days of your business.

Cash Flow Statement. This looks at the cash inflow and cash outflow of a business. Overall, the Cash Flow Statement can be seen as something that amounts to the net balance in your bank or it can be something that is forecast into the future. As the saying goes, 'Cash is King' and the more cash a company has available, the more likely it is to survive and prosper.

Cost of sales (COS) or **cost of goods sold** (COGS). Your COS (manufacturers know it as COGS) is the cost of actually making the sale. So if you are a recruitment company, it is the recruitment consultant's costs that would be included in your COS. This includes their salary as well as commission. If you are a manufacturer of woollen hats, then the cost of the woolly hats are going to be your COGS. The salaries of the people that actually make the woolly hats also form part of your COGS. However, your receptionist or security staff who have nothing to do with making or selling the woolly hats, will NOT form part of your COGS.

Creditors/accounts payable. Creditors, also known as Accounts Payable (AP), this is a name given to all the suppliers you or your company owe money to.

Current assets (short-term assets). These are assets that are easily convertible into cash. So, this would include stock (or inventory), debtors (see debtors), money in the bank, and any cash that the company currently holds.

Current liabilities (short-term liabilities). This is money that the company owes in the short-term. The short-term in this context means within 12 months. Items contained in current (or short term) liabilities include money owed to:

- Creditors
- Tax agencies
- Banks i.e. loans

Debtors / accounts receivable. Debtors, also known as Accounts Receivable (AR), is a name for any customers that owe you or your company money.

Depreciation. This is the value lost over time of a tangible fixed asset item. So a vehicle bought today will have gone down in value in a year's time. The amount that it has gone down by is called depreciation and appears as a cost in the financials.

Direct costs. (see Cost of sales)

Equity. This is the amount of an asset that you actually own. So if you own 15% of your house, and the mortgage is for 85%, then your equity is 15%. If you own 100% of your company, then you have 100% equity in your company.

Fixed assets (long-term assets). These are assets that you need to have to help you in the everyday running of operations in the business. Long-term assets include: machinery (used for manufacturing etc.), vehicles, and buildings etc. These are assets that are not regularly replaced, and which you will tend to use for more than one year.

Fixed costs. These are costs that stay the same over a period of time (usually a year) and do not change, regardless of how many goods/services are produced or delivered. So fixed costs have to be paid regardless of the level of activity being undertaken. Items that are classified as fixed costs include: rent, rates and salaried employees who are back-office staff.

For example, the training department rent a building where they carry out their training. In this building there are five rooms specifically allocated to them for training. If they only have two classes on this week, then the other three rooms will remain empty. The training department would still have to pay the rent for the other three rooms regardless of whether they have people in them or not.

Another example might be if you are a manufacturing company making 25,000 woolly hats a year and the rental cost of the building is £10,000 per year, fixed for three years. But if the next year they made 50,000 hats whilst using the same amount of space, the rent still costs £10,000 per year. So the overall fixed cost has stayed the same, regardless of how many hats were produced.

Gross profit. This is the amount left over from your sales when your cost of sales have been taken out. It helps you to understand where you can improve your production processes.

Gross profit margin. This is the gross profit amount, but expressed as a percentage. And this is expressed as a percentage in relation to the overall sales. This figure helps you to compare your performance to your competitors. So the formula is:

$$\frac{\text{Gross Profit}}{\text{Sales}} \times 100 = \text{gross profit margin}$$

So if your total sales are 150, and your gross profit is 100, then the gross profit margin is:

$$\frac{100}{150} \quad X \quad 100 \quad = 66.67\%$$

Indirect costs. These are costs that are difficult to assign to a specific cost unit and are, therefore, shared costs to a host of items. If you made widgets, indirect costs would be those costs that don't directly impact on making widgets. So it would be the receptionists' wages, rent, rates, security etc.

Long-term liabilities. This is a section of the Balance Sheet that shows all of a company's obligations which are due for longer than 12 months. Such obligations could include a mortgage where a mortgage is paid back over 25 or so years. Other loans which are due to be paid back beyond 12 months also come under this heading.

Mark up. This is the percentage increase on the cost of the product, which will then give the product its sales price. For example, if the cost of an item is £1.00 and you wanted to have a mark-up of 60%, then the sale price of the product is £1.60.

Net profit. This is the amount left over from your sales when both your direct AND indirect costs have been taken out. This is commonly known as the final figure that tells us how much the company has made.

Net profit margin. Similar to the gross profit margin, the net profit margin is basically the net profit amount, but expressed as a percentage. It too is a useful figure that helps you compare performance against your competitors. The formula for this is:

$$\frac{\text{Net Profit}}{\text{Sales}} \quad X \quad 100 \quad = \text{net profit margin}$$

If your total sales are 150, and your net profit is 75, then the net profit margin is:

$$\frac{75}{150} \quad X \quad 100 \quad = 50\%$$

Non-operating expenses. These are expenses that are one-off costs or come outside the normal running of the business. Such costs would include interest payments on loans or re-organisation costs that have been incurred, e.g. following a re-structure in the business

Non-operating revenue. Interest earned on money deposits could be classified as non-operating revenue. Or maybe the business sold off some of its old equipment and generated income this way. This is classified as non-operating revenue as you are selling one-off items that come outside of your normal business activity.

Operating expenses. These are all the costs that help you run your business. Operating expenses may also be seen as indirect costs. Your receptionist, finance department and Human Resources department are not directly making or selling your woolly hats, but they are still important to the overall running of your business. They would come under the category of operating expenses.

Operating profit. This is the profit that has been generated when the operating expenses have been deducted from the gross profit. This measure of efficiency is important because it helps us understand how profitable a company's core business is.

Profit and Loss Account (also known as the income statement). This is a financial statement that summarises the performance of a business over a set period of time. It looks at the income the business has generated and takes away the overall expenses which will then leave us with a profit or loss.

Sales. Also commonly known as income, revenue or turnover. This is the term used for all the 'money' you are bringing in when you sell a product or service. So, if you sell a single woolly hat for £5, and it costs you £2 to make it, the sale is recorded as £5.

Semi-variable costs. This is a cross between fixed and variable costs. So a portion will be fixed, and a portion will be variable. An example of a semi-variable cost could be a telephone bill. You may have the monthly fixed bill for the telephone line and a variable monthly bill for the calls made.

Stock (inventory). This includes items of value that a business has in its possession that are ready to be sold, or is being made ready to be sold. Such items could include:

- finished items or products (that are ready to be sold)

- raw materials (that are in the process of being converted into finished items)

Variable costs. These are costs that are directly linked to levels of activity in a business. Costs that are classified as variable could include costs for raw materials. For example, if we are a manufacturer making woolly hats, then the amount of material (i.e. wool) we use would depend on how many hats we are producing.

Working capital. This looks at a company's ability to pay off its immediate debts by looking at all the items that can be quickly converted into cash. It does this by comparing the current assets of a business against its current liabilities. The theory goes that as long as the current assets are more than the current liabilities, then the company has a much better chance of surviving.

The formula is:

Working capital = current assets – current liabilities

About the Author

Zahoor Bargir is a qualified accountant who worked at PricewaterhouseCoopers before venturing out as a consultant. He has led teams at start-ups as well as at FTSE 100 companies. He has a unique talent for making things simple and specialises in training non-finance professionals on the wonders of finance.

Zahoor is an accomplished Finance Trainer and is also a mentor to many aspiring young finance professionals and entrepreneurs.

zahoor@companybasix.com
www.companybasix.com